Praise for
THE SEEKER, THE SEARCH, THE SACRED

"Guy Finley probes in this book the many doorways into a new consciousness and opens up to his readers a vision of what human beings are capable of becoming."

> —JOHN SHELBY SPONG, retired Episcopal Bishop, author of *Reclaiming the Bible for a Non-Religious World*

"The timeless quotes from diverse traditions found within this book represent humanity's deepest spiritual aspirations. May they reach the hearts and souls of people everywhere."

> —ROBERT "SKIP" BACKUS, Chief Executive Officer, The Omega Institute

"*The Seeker, the Search, the Sacred* is a very wise book, filled with inspiration to help you dramatically improve your life. I highly recommend it."

> —DANIEL G. AMEN, MD, New York Times best-selling author of *Change Your Brain, Change Your Life* and *Healing the Hardware of the Soul*

"Guy Finley's mastery of the modern parable allows him to subtly plant and tend seeds of conscious awakening deep within the heart and mind of the reader without the ego's resistance. Then we suddenly realize that we are awakening from an unintended slumber, and our feet are firmly on the path we have been secretly seeking. An important work for all who suspect they have been asleep and are yearning for a more authentic, sacred life. We are waking."

> —REV. RIC BEATTIE, Renaissance Unity, Warren, Michigan

"The Seeker, the Search, the Sacred is a wise, very accessible, and enjoyable guide to the well-springs of the spiritual life to be found deep within ourselves . . . This beautiful book will be a great resource for all readers."

> —DR. MARIA REIS HABITO, international program director, Museum of World Religions

"The Seeker, the Search, the Sacred is a giant leap for mankind—definitely more important than the footprint left on the moon! With this monumental undertaking, Guy has reminded each of us that we are Love and that all the religions agree, at their root, that this is the Truth of us all."

> —DR. MICHAEL RYCE, Director, Khabouris Manuscript Foundation, author of *Why Is This Happening To Me . . . Again!*

"I whole-heartedly endorse *The Seeker, the Search, the Sacred* with confidence that it will open the reader's eyes to the beauty and majesty of Eternal Truth."

> —DESI ARNAZ JR., actor and producer

"Guy Finley invokes the Sacred within all of us with his insightful storytelling, echoing and joining the great masters of the search. He challenges us, as seekers of truth and happiness, to make the inner journey."

—BABA RAMPURI, author of *Autobiography of a Sadhu, a Journey into Mystic India*

"Throughout his prolific career Guy Finley's works have shown countless readers and workshop participants the way to develop the uniqueness that the Creator endowed in them and in each of us. In his latest book, *The Seeker, the Search, the Sacred*, he affords his audience the opportunity to go beyond reading and to participate in the individual and collective human development on a global scale."

—DON WHITTECAR, CEO, The Emergent Institute

"Coalesced from the sages and thinkers over a 5,000 year period, *The Seeker, the Search, the Sacred* provides the basis for a new network of how 'interacting activists' can work together on issues of interfaith unity to provide a positive future. Here is a look at how quantum mind and spirit can work together to build a global commons. Let us work together to engage the next quantum leap!"

—J. J. HURTAK, PhD, Academy for Future Science, author of *The Keys of Enoch*

"So much more than a profound and powerful collection of spiritual quotations, in *The Seeker, the Search, the Sacred*, Guy Finley has gifted us with an insightful work to slowly savor; a road map to assist us on that great and mysterious road trip, our journey to ourselves. I most strongly recommend it!"

—GREG WILLSON, Co-editor, *Cultivate Life!* magazine

"The Seeker, the Search, the Sacred is a wonderful work of mastery, and a must read for any aspirant."

—Greg Voisen, Founder, Inside Personal Edge

"I enthusiastically endorse *The Seeker, the Search, the Sacred.* People will keep this book on their nightstands as a permanent Dreamweaver and source of inspiration. Readers will be able to inspire both themselves and others to accomplish great things."

—MURRAY W. NABORS, PHD, Dean of Liberal Arts and Sciences, Missouri Western State University, author of *The Magical Dozen*

"It is impossible to convey the wisdom, depth, and magnitude of Guy Finley's new project, *The Seeker, the Search, the Sacred.* Ultimately, all healing—within us and between us and the planet—is about reconnection with the Divine. We are all on the same journey home to our true self. This masterful new work gives hope to a deeply divided planet."

—STEPHEN DANIEL, PHD, FPPR, founder of QuantumTechniques.com

THE SEEKER

THE SEARCH

THE SACRED

ALSO BY GUY FINLEY

The Courage to Be Free

The Essential Laws of Fearless Living

Let Go and Live in the Now

The Secret of Letting Go

Apprentice of the Heart

365 Days to Let Go

Design Your Destiny

The Lost Secrets of Prayer

Letting Go a Little Bit at a Time

Seeker's Guide to Self-Freedom

Freedom From the Ties That Bind

The Meditative Life

Secrets of Being Unstoppable

Being Fearless and Free

Liberate Your Self

Secrets of Spiritual Success

The Majestic Life

For a complete list of the author's works, visit
www.guyfinley.org, where you can also join the free Key
Lesson Club to receive weekly insights by email.

THE
SEEKER
THE
SEARCH
THE
SACRED

JOURNEY TO THE GREATNESS WITHIN

GUY FINLEY

WEISERBOOKS
San Francisco, CA / Newburyport, MA

First published in 2011 by Weiser Books, an imprint of
Red Wheel/Weiser, LLC
665 Third Street, Suite 400
San Francisco, CA 94107
www.redwheelweiser.com

ISBN: 978-1-57863-502-3

Library of Congress Cataloging-in-Publication Data is available upon
request.

Cover design by Jim Warner
Interior by Maureen Forys, Happenstance Type-O-Rama
Typeset in Elysium with Futura Pro and Trajan Pro

Printed in the United States of America
MAL

10 9 8 7 6 5 4 3 2 1

The paper used in this publication meets the minimum requirements of
the American National Standard for Information Sciences—Permanence of
Paper for Printed Library Materials Z39.48-1992 (R1997).

This book is part of a much larger story—The OneJourney Project—which seeks to spread the message of our common celestial bond across the globe. To learn more about this important work in progress, and how you can participate in the great promise it holds for all humankind, visit OneJourney.net.

CONTENTS

SPECIAL THANKS

A book like this—whose materials were gathered and refined over many years—required many helping hands. Some of the people who were instrumental during its inception are no longer with us in body, but their contribution goes on . . . as does my appreciation for the sacrifices I know they made to help this project along the way.

My heartfelt thanks to Robert DeJohn, Denise Welch, Sara Robinson, and Dr. Ellen Dickstein for all their patient efforts to help me organize this material in its many incarnations over the years.

Much thanks to the great team of editors at Red Wheel/Weiser, including Addie Johnson, but especially to my publisher, Jan Johnson. It was she who encouraged me to complete this project, and who coordinated the editorial efforts leading up to the birth of this book.

Lastly, for her ability to see what I would not during the development of any new work, and then to never expect less than the very best I can do, my deepest gratitude goes to my friend, partner in life, and wife, Patricia. Her eyes are always the first and the last to look at any work that I do, and her thoughts were instrumental in the final way this material is presented.

—GF

DEDICATION

I n one respect, this book is *nearly 5,000 years in the making!* However, drama aside—and on a far more rea-sonable scale of time—the truth is I began collecting the timeless ideas for this book more than thirty years ago. It was back then that good fortune brought me into contact with author and philosopher Vernon Howard. During the first year of the fourteen years I spent under his kind and clear interior guidance (until his passing in 1992), I fell deeply in love with one of his early works entitled *The Mystic Masters Speak*.

This book, penned by a modern-day master, repre-sented a vast compilation of great quotations carefully categorized into an extensive list of wide-ranging top-ics. The scope of subjects ran the gamut of human expe-rience—from the nature of success, releasing negative states, embracing higher love and happy human relation-ships all the way to realizing one's place and responsibil-ity in the order of creation.

Above all else, this collection of hundreds of indi-vidual spiritual gems made evident the existence of a single truth, a treasure greater than the sum of its parts:

within everyone there dwells a living Light, a conscious-ness whose love and compassion never flag; it is a timeless intelligence whose wisdom, once awakened, provides both explanation and solution for all of the suffering and sor-row that we see taking place around . . . and within us.

Without knowing how, the truth behind this revela-tion made something else abundantly clear: finding this higher life is not meant to be the exception to the rule; it *is* the rule for anyone willing to undertake the interior journey.

Slowly, but with an ever-increasing certainty—like seeing a great mountain as it appears from out of a lift-ing fog—my mind could see undreamed-of possibilities emerging from this body of new knowledge. And from somewhere deep within me a single question took form, one that has stayed with me to this very day:

> *What if timeless ideas like these were introduced to the whole world in such a way as to reveal their secret story? Could the light of these truths—the hope and promise they hold about our own latent higher possibilities—help liberate us from the host of fears that hold our consciousness hostage?*

Imagine the end of all forms of fanaticism born of imagined differences, the beginning of a new order of peace created from the collective understanding that *all* beings on earth share a common purpose.

And so I set myself to this task of trying to seed these timeless ideas into the world by creating a syndicated newspaper column by the same title as the book.

Fast-forward eighteen months! As the fates would have it, the best I could do at the time was to "fumble and bumble" my way through creating a very limited, highly localized syndicated newspaper column based on the book's content; and, as things turned out, this was a task doomed to fail before it began.

Simply put, I learned an invaluable lesson: while most people proclaim their wish to be free, hardly anyone is willing to undertake the serious interior work required to have their wish granted! It became painfully clear: our deeply conditioned social wish, for a constant and familiar sense of self, takes precedence over our latent spiritual need to be made anew. From discoveries such as these often springs a seed. . . .

Perhaps it was, in part, this summary rejection of what I loved so dearly that spawned in me the idea that is now this book. I remember thinking that "one day" I too would undertake the same task as did Mr. Howard—only perhaps I could find another way and create a wholly different kind of vehicle that would help tell, and then explain, the unspoken story hidden for millennia within the words of the world's greatest masters.

This book—my attempt to honor and reveal this one underlying reality behind all truth teachings—is dedicated to the master teacher Vernon Howard. His tireless work and endless compassion helped make possible the understanding that anyone who so desires can, in this lifetime, realize a wholly new and immortal order of being.

Thank you, VH, for everything . . .

INTRODUCTION

SEEDS OF FIRE, FOOTPRINTS IN THE SAND

Small is the number of people who see with their eyes and think with their minds.

—ALBERT EINSTEIN

Whenever our world is altered for the better, it does so for only one reason: somewhere, in some place, someone (just like you and me) is suddenly "changed." In the blink of an eye there comes an unexpected, but long-hoped-for visitation; a totally new idea appears in a mind that's been preparing just for its arrival, and a marriage takes place between *what has been* and *what yet may be*.

Like stars that dot the evening sky, our history is filled with bright moments such as these, where something altogether new is given birth; from them come the discoveries that change the world we know. But, as we are about to see, there also exists the possibility of an altogether different kind of marriage, one whose con-summation changes the very nature of the individual within whom that union takes place. In moments of such

interior brilliance, useless forms and limited beliefs—
along with the old gods of their origin—are reduced to
ashes. Here is one account of an illumination, reported
by German author Malwida von Meysenbug:

> *I was alone upon the seashore as all these thoughts flowed over
> me, liberating and reconciling; and now again, as once before
> in distant days in the Alps of Dauphine, I was impelled to kneel
> down, this time before the illimitable ocean, symbol of the infi-
> nite. I prayed as I've never prayed before, and knew now what
> prayer really is: to return from the solitude of individuation
> into the consciousness of unity with all that is, to kneel down
> as one passes away, and to rise up as one imperishable. Earth,
> heaven, and sea resounded as in one vast world encircling har-
> mony. It was as if the chorus of all the great who ever lived were
> about me. I felt myself one with them, and it appeared as if I
> heard the greeting: "Thou too belongst to the company of those
> who overcome."*

—RICHARD BUCKE, *Cosmic Consciousness*

Anyone graced by such an illumination sees the world
anew, from a fresh and holy perspective. Greater powers—
the shared presence of higher principles once considered
impossible—are recognized as natural, if not common,
rights. And like ripples radiating out from the center of a
pond into which a stone has been thrown, the force of this
awakened new perception—this realization of what has

always been one's higher possibility—establishes a new reality. Everything is changed, forever . . .

Although clearly in scale from minor to momentous insights, "aha!" moments like these appear in the life of everyone; but, for the most part, the major changes they herald go largely unnoticed save for the circle of friends or family whose lives are ultimately impacted as a result of such awakenings.

Nevertheless, every period of recorded history reports the arrival of what must be considered certain "game-changing" ideas, the advent of some unique insight whose appearance serves to transform the consciousness of the world itself. Of course, revelations such as these occur in *all* fields of endeavor. Like individual raindrops that feed our streams and rivers, it is new ideas that nourish and sustain the growth of science, art, and the humanities. Yet, seen aright, all that grows out of these varied branches flows, as it does, from out of one vast unseen ocean: self-knowledge. In his book, *Walden,* the words of Henry David Thoreau strengthen this finding:

> *Men esteem Truth remote, in the outskirts of the system, behind the farthest star, before Adam and after the last man. In eternity there is indeed something true and sublime. But all these times and places and occasions are now and here. God Himself culminates in the present moment, and will never be more divine in the lapse of all ages.*

Every truth ever discovered—each new light that will ever burn bright—already exists in our consciousness. All we will ever know and share about love, humility, compassion, and sacrifice—the secrets that will reveal and then resolve old sorrows—awaits us within ourselves. Hidden in this truth is our great promise, both as individuals and as a race of beings.

In this book, I call these timeless ideas that ignite and stir us to remember our forgotten spiritual heritage "seeds of fire." And even as the smallest mustard seed holds within itself the potential for a great vine, branches, and much fruit, so do higher ideas hold a threefold power that's unleashed as soon as it makes contact with the soil of a fertile mind. This three-in-one power is:

1. *Discrimination:* the ability to discern what is true from what is false.

2. *Intention:* the will to act upon and clarify one's discoveries.

3. *Illumination:* the realization of a new order of being freed from the bondage of self-induced limitation.

Let's illustrate with an example that shows how these stages are always present whenever we realize a new truth about ourselves. As should be clear, all of us have known—and grown through—one form or another of the events that follow.

One day, in the midst of that misery born of being in some kind of abusive relationship, a new idea enters into the mind of the woman involved. A simple truth rocks her world: *patterns can't change themselves!* And by the light of this one insight she discerns, clearly, the shadow of the false hope to which she had been clinging: neither blaming her partner for her pain nor hoping he will change has altered a thing. Now she knows: to remain where she is guarantees she will remain a victim.

The more she realizes the truth of her untenable situation, the clearer it becomes: in spite of her fear over what "may be," *she must act.* An inescapable intention is born that gives birth to a glad day: she walks out of her old ways and into the new life just ahead.

A short time later—perhaps over a quiet cup of tea, or maybe seated on a park bench, sharing the joy of watching dogs at play—out of nowhere a "light" appears in her mind. It comes in the form of a simple, but grand realization: *Only when one is comfortable, content with being alone, can one be true to another.* And with the dawning of this higher self-understanding comes an unexpected new order of self-confidence. For now she knows something else: *Never again will she be tempted to accept anything less than the kind of love that harms no one and that nurtures everyone!*

Where does the strength of this uncompromising wisdom, heralded by an entirely new order of compassion, come from? The brilliant 20th-century physicist, mystic, and Nobel Prize winner, Erwin Schrodinger, offers us a surprising answer—a "seed of fire"—bright with promise.

> *It is not possible that this unity of knowledge, feeling and choice which you call your own should have sprung into being from nothingness at a given moment not so long ago; rather this knowledge, feeling and choice are essentially eternal and unchangeable and numerically one in all men, nay in all sensitive beings. But not in this sense—that you are a part, a piece, of an eternal, infinite being, or aspect or modification of it, as in Spinoza's pantheism. For we should have the same baffling question: which part, which aspect are you? What objectively, differentiates it from the others? No, but inconceivable as it seems to ordinary reason, you—and all other conscious beings as such—are all in all. Hence this life of yours which you are living is not merely a piece of the entire existence, but is, in a certain sense, the WHOLE; only this whole is not so constituted that it can be surveyed in one single glance.*

—Erwin Schrodinger, *My View of the World*

Who can read thoughts like these and not feel something of the depth and breadth of the revelation behind them? This intimate quality of communion—the momentary sharing of a timeless luminescence—is one of the earmarks of any seed of fire. Soul-stirring insights such as this—that reach in and remind us of nobility lost—illuminate the skies of passing time, like stars on a moonless night. Yet, by their far-flung light, we don't just read the history of our possibilities; we are also made aware of a latent interior greatness that awaits us *now*. This means that regardless of when in time, or where on earth, one of these truths appears, its effect is always the same. By its deft touch, "the sleeper awakens," and the meaning of our life takes on a whole new magnitude.

A kind of spiritual birth takes place when our consciousness first becomes aware of itself. Something *is* born in us in that same moment; there's a distinct sense that within us lays buried "a pearl of great price." Faint as it may be, we perceive the presence of an immeasurable, if not divine, life whose possibilities are somehow recognized as being the same as our own. But with this great promise revealed comes also the inevitable birth of a new kind of longing.

Imagine someone who has lived out her entire life completely alone on a small island. As a result of her condition, she has no awareness whatsoever that anyone—or anything else—like her exists.

Then, one day, while exploring the most distant part of the island, she rounds a point and stops dead in her tracks. Before her, stretching into the distance—and around the other side of the point where the rising tide has all but erased any evidence of them—is a set of footprints in the sand!

Stunned by her discovery, her thoughts race to a standstill. She *knows* it wasn't she who made these footprints, because her own tracks lead right up to them. Slowly the evidence mounts into something unthinkable: though these strange prints are clearly similar in shape and form to her own, they're unmistakably larger, wider, and leave a deeper impression.

Like someone suddenly shaken awake from a deep dream, her mind struggles to make sense of what's real and what's not; even so, she's aware of one thing for sure: *she is not alone!* Something has happened from which there will be no turning back; and from this point forward, both fearful and attracted to what she may find, she spends all of her waking hours in search of the one who left the footprints in the sand. *When the sleeper awakens, the seeker is born.*

Whenever, through our exploration of life, we come upon some "seed of fire"—some new thought or insight that awakens us to a part of ourselves unknown only a moment before—we realize that *we are not alone.* These sometimes shocking moments make two things clear at once:

First, someone "out there"—whose "footprints" we have stumbled upon—knows us better than we know ourselves, for they have awakened us to a truth about ourselves that we didn't know a moment before. And, for having now been introduced to what amounts to a higher level of our own awareness, we also receive another gift beyond description: the realization that within us already lives a body of timeless wisdom that is more who we are than anything we could have ever imagined ourselves to be. But even this discovery, as great as it is, is just one of the diamonds to be uncovered along the way. Though the treasure of true self-knowledge is immeasurable, here is a brief summary of what we've already come to see about its timeless nature:

The new self-understanding for which we search *is already a part of the seeker*, as it's always found there, within us, or not at all. And further, *that it is the Sacred itself that secretly initiates the search!* There is but one timeless Self seemingly divided into three parts: "The Seeker, the Search, the Sacred."

This book offers the reader a collection of universal spiritual quotations—personal favorites—I have collected over the last thirty-five years. They have been carefully divided into three distinct categories, within which they are presented chronologically—from the earliest to the most recent. This select method of presentation is, itself, as much a part of the story I hope to tell as the material being presented through it.

Can a collection of hundreds of thoughts—spread out across a vast expanse of space and time—spoken world-over by thousands of different voices—tell a single coherent story? The answer is an unqualified "Yes!"—but only when each of these seeds of fire is realized for what it is: the expressed reflection of the divine mind from which they radiate, not unlike the light from the sun which reveals itself in the glimmer of a thousand diamonds as they dance upon the sea.

SECTION ONE

THE SEEKER

THE INVISIBLE
NEED IN EVERY SEED

There is a very old idea that, as best can be determined, comes to us from the days of the early Christian Desert Fathers. In six concise words it touches upon a certain fact of human nature that even volumes of books would prove unable to express any better: "Fish swim, birds fly . . . man prays."

In other words, it's the nature of fish to glide through water, for birds to soar through open skies, because they are at home there. Sea and sky, accordingly, are the worlds of their origin, where they belong, the place they are free. But where is our true home? What is the nature of that place where our original self is one with its longing to explore its own deepest possibilities, and where discovering the treasures waiting there is the same as fulfilling our purpose for being? What world is there for us where *our* essential nature—and its right to live free—is one and the same?

We're granted a quick glimpse of this secret destination in these spirit-filled lines from American poet Walt Whitman's classic work, *Leaves of Grass*.

Would you sound below the restless ocean of the entire world? Would you know the dissatisfaction? the urge and spur of every life; the something never still'd—never entirely gone? the invisible need of every seed? It is the central urge in every atom to return to its divine source and origin, however distant.

In the first of these four lines, we're asked a vital question: is there a part of us that longs to know—that's willing to seek out—what lies hidden just beneath the thought-tossed surface of ourselves? If our answer is "Yes," then Mr. Whitman goes on to suggest what awaits us there in that great, undiscovered country of our innermost Self. In summary, he asks: Are we willing to bear—to share in the being of an unceasing creation—to embody what he calls *"the invisible need of every seed"*? And then, for those who still affirm their wish to drink from that eternal cup of life, he pours out the rest. We learn, at once, why seekers of all ages have always felt this "central urge" to merge with the highest part of themselves: *we are called . . . to "return to our divine source and origin."*

It may be difficult to see at first, like a pearl washed ashore nestled into a bed of small pebbles, but hidden within this last idea is a beautiful spiritual fact: those who feel this call—who "hunger and thirst after righteousness"—are not alone in their search to find their way back home. A simple example proves this point:

A child at play in the yard can't see the concerned parent whose voice calls out to him, "It's getting dark, time to come in!" And yet, even that small child understands that although the parent isn't in view, he's still there: unseen doesn't mean unreal. With this truth in mind, follow the logic of the next few ideas; your patient work to understand them will help open your eyes to the light of a new hope in things unseen.

No natural need can exist without that which has been created to directly answer it. For instance, a creature couldn't thirst for water if water didn't preexist its *need to drink*. This feeling of attraction that we have—whether to take a drink of water or connect with the world above us—is proof of the existence of *two* parties. First is the part of us that feels this draw, and then *there is by necessity something acting upon us* to create the longing itself. As paradoxical as it may seem, if we are moved to seek the Divine, it's because the Divine *is calling us*! Let's pause here to see how this celestial need expresses itself through some simple examples that are common to all of us: Where does our longing for someone to love originate? Is it not with the awakening of an internal force urging us to explore and experience the deepest parts of ourselves? When we say—or feel toward another—"You complete me," what we're really saying is something like "Through you I've realized parts of myself I wouldn't have known even existed; *you have helped introduce me to who I really am."*

Perhaps we've a yearning to learn how to paint, write poetry, climb a mountain, or become a chef. We are drawn to that pursuit—whatever its nature—for much the same reason we search for a lover. Something in us knows that it is only through this relationship that we will be introduced to—*awakened to*—our own higher possibilities.

C. S. Lewis, the great author, essayist, and Christian apologist, supports this important finding in *The Problem of Pain*:

> *All the things that have ever deeply possessed your soul have been but hints of it—tantalizing glimpses, promises never quite fulfilled, echoes that died away just as they caught your ear. But if IT should really become manifest—if there ever came an echo that did not die away but swelled into the sound itself— you would know it. Beyond all possibility of doubt you would say, "Here at last is the thing I was made for." We cannot tell each other about it. It is the secret signature of each soul, the incommunicable and unappeasable want, the thing we desired before we met our wives or made our friends or chose our work, and which we shall still desire on our deathbeds, when the mind no longer knows wife or friend or work.*

The need for whatever it may be that we're drawn to is the *yet to be realized presence within us* of that very thing to which we are drawn. This means that no matter how distant seems our guiding star, or how isolated we may feel in our journey toward its light, these higher truths we're learning would have us know otherwise; **we are not alone**. Even more importantly, just as a small filing of iron *must* fly to the magnet that pulls upon it, so too must those who are drawn to the Divine eventually answer its call.

In the following section, you will read the innermost thoughts and feelings of inspired seekers who have gone before you. Some names you may know; others you will be glad to meet! But as you journey along with them in the pages that follow, sharing in their discoveries and discouragements, one thing should grow increasingly clear: the Spirit that called them—that awakened their hearts, and quickened their minds—so that they might have "eyes to see, and ears to hear"—is the same spirit calling you. These individuals came to know, as will you, the truth that sets us free: *There is but one seeker, one search, and one sacred intelligence awakening you with its call.*

THE MASTERS SPEAK
OF THE SEEKER

Wisdom is sweeter than honey, brings more joy than wine,
illumines more than the sun, is more precious than jewels.
She causes the ears to hear and the heart to comprehend.

—QUEEN MAKEDA (1000 BCE, Ethiopia)

The Lord hath poured out upon you the spirit of deep sleep,
and hath closed your eyes.

—ISAIAH, OLD TESTAMENT (700 BCE)

If you persist in trying
To attain what is never attained
If you persist in making effort
To obtain what effort cannot get;
If you persist in reasoning
About what cannot be understood,
You will be destroyed

By the very thing you seek.
To know when to stop
To know when you can get no further
By your own action,
This is the right beginning!

—Lao Tzu (ca. 570–490 BCE, China)

He who knoweth not what he ought to know is a brute beast
among men; he that knoweth no more than he hath need of,
is a man among brute beasts; and he that knoweth all that
may be known, is as a God among men.

—Pythagoras (569–475 BCE, Greece)

The intelligible substance, if it is drawn near to God, has
power over itself. . . . If it falls away, it chooses the corporeal
world and in that way becomes subject to necessity which
rules the Kosmos.

—Ioannis Stobaei (500 BCE, Macedonia)

Thinking about sense objects
Will attach you to sense objects;
Grow attached, and you become addicted;
Thwart your addiction, it turns to anger;
Be angry, and you confuse your mind;

Confuse your mind, you forget the lesson of experience;
Forget experience, you lose discrimination;
Lose discrimination, and you miss life's
Only purpose.

—BHAGAVAD GITA (500–200 BCE, India)

God made the senses turn outward, man therefore looks outward, not into himself. Sometimes a daring man has looked
round and found himself. Then he is immortal!

—KATHA UPANISHAD (4th c. BCE, India)

Each one of us is made up of ten thousand different and suc-
cessive states, a scrap-heap of units, a mob of individuals.

—PLUTARCH (45–125, Greece)

This people's heart is waxed gross, and their ears are dull of
hearing and their eyes have closed, lest haply they should perceive with their eyes and hear with their ears, and understand
with their heart.

—ST. MATTHEW, NEW TESTAMENT (55–60)

God made man so that He should seek the Lord.

—ACTS, NEW TESTAMENT (55–95)

When therefore we are hindered, or disturbed, or grieved, let us seek the cause rather in ourselves than elsewhere. It is the action of an uninstructed person to lay the fault of his own bad condition upon others; of a partly instructed person, to lay the fault on himself; and of one perfectly instructed, neither on others, nor on himself.

—EPICTETUS (55–135, Phrygia, Asia Minor)

Now . . . Faith is a conviction of the reality of the things which we do not see. Through faith we understand that the world came into being and still exists at the command of God, so that what is seen does not owe its existence to that which is visible.

—HEBREWS, NEW TESTAMENT (60–100)

When you know yourselves, then you will be known and you will understand that you are children of the living father. But if you do not know yourselves, then you dwell in poverty, and you are poverty.

—GOSPEL OF THOMAS (60–140, Egypt)

Ye shall know the truth, and the truth shall make you free.

—ST. JOHN, NEW TESTAMENT (ca. 90)

Charity bears all things, is long suffering in all things. There is nothing mean to charity, nothing arrogant. Charity knows no schism, does not rebel, does all things in concord. In charity all the elect of God have been made perfect.

—CLEMENT OF ROME (d. 101 CE, Italy)

Fall in love with Wisdom and she will keep you . . . put her around you, and she will exalt you; honor her that she may embrace you. . . .

—ORIGEN (185–254, Egypt)

To know goodness is not sufficient to reach blessedness; if one does not put goodness into practice with works. Piety towards God is actually the beginning of knowledge.

—DIDYMUS THE BLIND (313–398, Greece)

Thou hast formed us for Thyself, and our hearts are restless till they find rest in Thee.

—ST. AUGUSTINE (354–430, Algeria)

This thing we tell of can never be found by seeking, yet only seekers find it.

—BAYAZID BASTAMI (804–874, Persia)

The whole world is you. Yet you keep thinking there is something else.

> — Hsüeh-Feng I-ts'un (822–908, China)

When you are deluded and full of doubt, even a thousand books of scripture are not enough. When you have realized understanding, even one word is too much.

> —Fen-Yang (947–1024, Ancient Taiyuan)

"Has the road an end or not?" He answered: "The road has an end, but the stations have no end, for the journey is twofold, one to God and one in God."

> —Fariduddin Attar (ca. 1142–ca. 1220, Nishapur, Khorasan)

Don't grieve for what doesn't come.
Some things that don't happen
Keep disasters from happening.

> —Jalal al-Din Rumi (ca. 1207–1273, Balkh, Persia)

I remember that in the time of childhood I was very religious; I rose in the night, was punctual in the performance of my devotions, and abstinent. One night I had been sitting in the presence of my father, not having closed my eyes during the whole time, and with the holy Koran in my embrace, whilst numbers around us were asleep. I said to my father: "Not one of these lifteth up his head to perform his genuflexions, but they are all so fast asleep you would say they are dead." He replied: "Life of your father, it were better if thou also wert asleep than to be searching out the faults of mankind. The boaster sees nothing but himself, having a veil of conceit before his eyes. If he were endowed with an eye capable of discerning God, he would not discern any person weaker than himself.

—SAADI (ca. 1213–1292, Persia)

We are the cause of all our obstacles.

—MEISTER ECKHART (1260–ca. 1327, Thuringia)

The humble knowledge of thyself is a surer way to God than the deepest search after science.

—THOMAS A' KEMPIS (ca. 1380–1471, the Netherlands)

I laugh when I hear that the fish in the water are thirsty. You don't grasp the fact that what is most alive of all is inside your own house; and so you walk from one holy city to the next with a confused look!

—KABIR (1398–1518, India)

My unassisted heart is barren clay,
That of its native self can nothing feed:
Of Good and pious works Thou art the seed,
That quickens only where Thou sayest it may:
Unless Thou show to us Thine own true way
No man can find it: Father! Thou must lead.

—MICHELANGELO (1475–1564, Caprese, Tuscany)

Man does not know himself and does not know how to use the
energies hidden in him, nor does he know that he carries the
stars hidden in himself and that he is the microcosm, and thus
carries within him the whole firmament with all its influence.

—PARACELSUS (1493–1541, Switzerland)

Who seeks, and will not take when once 'tis offered, shall
never find it more.

—WILLIAM SHAKESPEARE (1564–1616, England)

Who overcomes by force, hath overcome but half his foe.

—JOHN MILTON (1608–1674, England)

Ah! knew we but the want we have of the grace and assistance of God, we should never lose sight of Him—no,

not for a moment. Believe me; make immediately a holy and firm resolution never more willfully to forget Him, and to spend the rest of your days in His sacred presence, deprived for the love of Him, if He thinks fit, of all consolations.

—BROTHER LAWRENCE (1611–1691, France)

There are only three types of people; those who have found God and serve him; those who have not found God and seek him, and those who live not seeking, or finding him. The first are rational and happy; the second unhappy and rational, and the third foolish and unhappy.

—BLAISE PASCAL (1623–1662, France)

Do not seek to follow in the footsteps of the wise. Seek what they sought.

—MATSUO BASHO (1644–1694, Iga Province, Japan)

It is very rare to find ground which produces nothing. If it is not covered with flowers, fruit trees, and grains, it produces briars and pines. It is the same with man; if he is not virtuous, he becomes vicious.

—JEAN DE LA BRUYÈRE (1645–1696, France)

But when people are told to seek God within, it is like telling them to go to another planet. What is farther away and more unknown than the bottom of your own heart?

—FRANÇOIS FENELON (1651–1715, France)

The greatest part of mankind . . . may be said to be asleep, and that particular way of life which takes up each man's mind, thoughts, and actions, may be very well called his particular dream. This degree of vanity is equally visible in every form and order of life. The learned and the ignorant, the rich and the poor, are all in the same state of slumber.

—WILLIAM LAW (1686–1761, England)

All that is needed for the triumph of evil is for good men to do nothing.

—EDMUND BURKE (1729–1797, Ireland)

We do not worship the Great Spirit as the white men do, but we believe that forms of worship do not matter to the Great Spirit; what pleases him is the offering of a sincere heart, and this is how we worship him. We do not want to destroy your religion or to take it from you. We want only to enjoy our own.

—CHIEF SA-GO-YE-WAT-HA, AKA CHIEF RED JACKET
(1750–1830, United States)

No bird soars too high, if he soars with his own wings.

—WILLIAM BLAKE (1757–1827, England)

The brave man is not he who feels no fear, for that were stupid and irrational, but he whose noble soul its fear subdues, and bravely dares the danger nature shrinks from.

—JOANNA BAILLIE (1762–1851, Scotland)

The aim of education should be to convert the mind into a living fountain, and not a reservoir. That which is filled by merely pumping in, will be emptied by pumping out.

—JOHN M. MASON (1770–1829, United States)

Man who man would be
Must rule the empire of himself; in it
Must be supreme, establishing his throne,
Of vanquished will, quelling the anarchy
Of hopes and fears, being himself alone.

—PERCY BYSSHE SHELLEY (1792–1822, England)

Seeking is not always the way to find.

—JULIUS HARE (1795–1855, Italy)

O thou that pinest in the imprisonment of the Actual, and criest bitterly to the gods for a kingdom wherein to rule and create, know this for a truth: the thing thou seekest is already here, "here or nowhere," couldst thou only see.

—THOMAS CARLYLE (1795–1881, Scotland)

We do not yet possess ourselves, and we know at the same time that we are much more.

—RALPH WALDO EMERSON
(1803–1882, United States)

To will what God wills is the only science that gives us rest.

—HENRY WADSWORTH LONGFELLOW
(1807–1882, United States)

Love is not an art like poetry, possible only to the few endowed for it, it is open and accessible to all.

—SØREN KIERKEGAARD (1813–1855, Denmark)

If you have built castles in the air, your work need not be lost; that is where they should be. Now put the foundations under them.

—HENRY DAVID THOREAU (1817–1862, United States)

What comfort, what strength, what economy there is in order—material order, intellectual order, moral order. To know where one is going and what one wishes—this is order; to keep one's word and one's engagements—again order; to have everything ready under one's hand to be able to dispose of all one's forces, and to have all one's means of whatever kind under command—still order; to discipline one's habits, one's efforts, one's wishes; to organize one's life, to distribute one's time . . . all this belongs to and is included in the word order. Order means light and peace, inward liberty and free command over oneself; order is power.

—HENRI AMIEL (1821–1881, Switzerland)

The man who seeks one thing in life, and but one,
May hope to achieve it before life be done;
But he who seeks all things, wherever he goes,
Only reaps from the hopes which around him he sows
A harvest of barren regrets.

—ROBERT BULWER-LYTTON (1831–1891, England)

"Who are YOU?" said the Caterpillar.

This was not an encouraging opening for a conversation. Alice replied, rather shyly, "I—I hardly know, sir, just at present—at least I know who I was when I got up this morning, but I think I must've been changed several times since then."

—LEWIS CARROLL (1832–1898, England)

The greatest works are done by the ones.—The hundreds do not often do much—the companies never; it is the units— the single individuals, that are the power and the might.— Individual effort is, after all, the grand thing.

—CHARLES HADDON SPURGEON (1834–1892, England)

The "resurrection" is not of the so-called dead, but of the living who are "dead" in the sense of never having entered upon true life.

—RICHARD MAURICE BUCKE (1837–1902, Canada)

The lure of the distant and the difficult is deceptive. The great opportunity is where you are.

—JOHN BURROUGHS (1837–1921, United States)

There are no rules here. We're trying to accomplish something.

—THOMAS EDISON (1847–1931, United States)

A Creed for Those Who Have Suffered:
I asked God for strength that I might achieve . . .
I was made weak that I might learn humbly to obey.
I asked for health that I might do greater things . . .

I was given infirmity that I might do better things.
I asked for riches that I might be happy ...
I was given poverty that I might be wise.
I asked for power that I might have the praise of men ...
I was given weakness that I might feel the need of God.
I asked for all things that I might enjoy life ...
I was given life that I might enjoy all things.
I got nothing that I asked for ...
but everything I had hoped for.
Almost despite myself, my unspoken prayers were answered.
I am among all men most richly blessed.

—UNKNOWN CONFEDERATE SOLDIER
(ca. 1862, United States)

It is only when everything, even love, fails that with a flash,
man finds out how vain, how dream-like is this world. Then
he catches a glimpse ... of the beyond. It is only by giving up
this world that the other comes; never through holding on to
this one.

—VIVEKANANDA (1863–1902, India)

Religion is the first thing and the last thing, and until a
man has found God and been found by God, he begins at no
beginning, he works to no end.

—H. G. WELLS (1866–1946, England)

The real voyage of discovery consists not in seeking new landscapes, but in having new eyes.

—MARCEL PROUST (1871–1922, France)

He who has gotten rid of the disease of "tomorrow" has a chance of achieving what he is here for.

—GEORGE GURDJIEFF (ca. 1872–1949, Caucasus region)

For one human being to love another human being: that is perhaps the most difficult task that has been entrusted to us, the ultimate task, the final test and proof, the work for which all other work is merely preparation.

—RAINER MARIA RILKE (1875–1926, Bohemia)

Christ would never have made the impression He did on His followers if He had not expressed something that was alive and active in their unconscious. Christianity would never have spread through the pagan world with such astonishing rapidity had its ideas not found an analogous psychic readiness to receive them. It is this fact which also makes it possible to say that whoever believes in Christ is not only contained in Him, but that Christ then dwells in the believer as the perfect man formed in the image of God.

—CARL JUNG (1875–1961, Switzerland)

Man has no permanent and unchangeable I. Every thought, every mood, every desire, every sensation says "I." Each time his I is different. Just now it was a thought, now it is a desire, now a sensation, now another thought, and so on, endlessly. Man is a plurality. Man's name is legion.

—P. D. OUSPENSKY (1878–1947, Russia)

There is no greater mystery than this, that we keep seeking reality though in fact we are reality. We think that there is something hiding reality and that this must be destroyed before reality is gained. How ridiculous!

—RAMANA MAHARSHI (1879–1950, Tiruchuzhi, Tamil Nadu)

A human being is part of the whole, called by us "Universe"; a part limited in time and space. He experiences himself, his thoughts, and feelings as something separated from the rest—a kind of optical delusion of his consciousness. This delusion is a kind of prison for us, restricting us to our personal desires and to affection for a few persons nearest to us. Our task must be to free ourselves from this prison by widening our circle of compassion to embrace all living creatures, and the whole of nature in its beauty.

—ALBERT EINSTEIN (1879–1955, Germany)

I long to accomplish a great and noble task; but it is my chief duty to accomplish small tasks as if they were great and noble.

—HELEN KELLER (1880–1968, United States)

The best and most beautiful things cannot be seen or even touched, they must be felt with the heart.

—HELEN KELLER (1880–1968, United States)

To win for himself a little more of the creative energy, he tirelessly develops his thought, dilates his heart, intensifies his external activity, for created beings must work if they would be yet further created.

—PIERRE TEILHARD DE CHARDIN (1881–1955, France)

Your pain is the breaking of the shell that encloses your understanding.

—KAHLIL GIBRAN (1883–1931, Lebanon)

I imagined that unity of being could be reached within the customary state of consciousness. I believed, in other words, that a radical change of being could take place as one was, merely through some adjustments. This is probably what most of us think, for we do not realize that in order to change anything in ourselves everything else must change, lest by trying to change one thing we create wrong results in other directions. Change of being is not a patchwork process.

—MAURICE NICOLL (1884–1953, Scotland)

All insight, all revelation, all illumination, all love, all that is genuine, all that is real, lies in now—and in the attempt to create now we approach the inner precincts, the holiest part of life. For in time all things are seeking completion, but in now all things are complete.

—MAURICE NICOLL (1884–1953, Scotland)

What a curious phenomenon it is that you can get men to die for the liberty of the world who will not make the little sacrifice that is needed to free themselves from their own individual bondage.

—BRUCE BARTON (1886–1967, United States)

Love between human beings springs from a desire to be made free of another world than one's own; every true communion of lovers is a mutual discovery and recognition: every passion is a passion for release, for that loss of one's self by which alone one gains life.

—GERALD BULLETT (1893–1958, England)

Happiness does not come into being when you seek it; it is a byproduct; it comes into being when there is goodness, when there is love, when there is no ambition, when the mind is quietly seeking out what is true.

—J. KRISHNAMURTI (1895–1986, India)

One must seek the shortest way and the fastest means to get back home—to turn the spark within into a blaze, to be merged in and to identify with that greater fire which ignited the spark.

—NITYANANDA (1896–1961, India)

Everyone of us has had experiences which we have not been able to explain: a sudden sense of loneliness, or a feeling of wonder or awe in the face of the universal vastness. Or we have had a fleeting visitation of light like an illumination from some other sun, giving us in a quick flash an assurance that we are from another world, that our origins are divine.

—A. W. TOZER (1897–1963, United States)

Life on earth is threatened today not by man's failure to love his fellow man but by his inability to love at all. Love untainted by egoism is to be found only in the rarest of the rare.

—J. G. BENNETT (1897–1974, England)

If we look at men in the mass, we must believe in the doctrine of fatalism. It applies to them; they are compelled by their environments, they struggle like animals to survive precisely because they are not too far removed from the animal kingdom. . . . They react like automatons. . . . Move like puppets out of the blind universal instincts of nature. But this is not the end of the story. It is indeed only its beginning. For here and there a man emerges from the herd who is becoming an individual, creatively making himself into a fully human being. For him each day is a fresh experience, each experience is unique, each tomorrow no longer the completely inevitable and quite foreseeable inheritance of all its yesterdays. From being enslaved by animality and fatality, he is becoming free in full humanity and creativity.

—PAUL BRUNTON (1898–1981, England)

For all who but strive, who will but use untried forces, unknown energies, there are ungathered riches, unheard harmonies, unwon crowns, yea, an unrevealed heaven.

—MARY E. BAIN (1898–unknown, United States)

He is marking time, and he lives and dies like one of the million things he produces. He thinks of God, instead of experiencing God.

—ERICH FROMM (1900–1980, Germany)

I think that what we're seeking is an experience of being alive, so that our life experiences on the purely physical plane will have resonances within our own innermost being and reality, so that we actually feel the rapture of being alive.

—JOSEPH CAMPBELL (1904–1987, United States)

We seek what one might call a relative omnipotence: the power to have everything we want, to enjoy everything we desire, to demand that all our wishes be satisfied and that our will should never be frustrated or opposed. It is the need to have everyone else bow to our judgment and accept our declarations as law. It is the insatiable thirst for recognition of the excellence which we so desperately need to find in ourselves to avoid despair. This claim to omnipotence, our deepest secret and our inmost shame, is in fact the source of all our sorrows, all our unhappiness, all our dissatisfactions, all our mistakes and deceptions.

—THOMAS MERTON (1915–1968, France)

Death is not the greatest loss in life. The greatest loss is what dies within us while we are alive.

—NORMAN COUSINS (1915–1990, United States)

What guarantee is there that the five senses, taken together, do cover the whole of possible existence? They cover simply our actual experience, our human knowledge of facts or events. There are gaps between the fingers; there are gaps between the senses. In these gaps is the darkness which hides the connection between things . . . this darkness is the source of our vague fear and anxiety, but also the home of the gods. They alone see the connections, the total relevance of everything that happens; that which now comes to us in bits and pieces, the "accidents" which exist only in our heads, in our limited perceptions.

—IDRIS PARRY (1916–2008, Wales)

In seeking truth you have to get both sides of a story.

—WALTER CRONKITE (1916–2009, United States)

Whatever you think appears in consciousness as a show. That's the way thought works to display its content, as a show of imagination. Therefore if you think the observer is separate from the observed, it's going to appear in consciousness as two different entities. The point is that the words will seem to be coming from the observer who knows, who sees, and therefore they are the truth, they are a description of the truth. That's the illusion.

—DAVID BOHM (1917–1992, United States)

The only sane thing to do with the world is to let it struggle with its own problems. You can do this only when seeing clearly that the world prefers to struggle painfully with its problems, never really wanting solutions.

—VERNON HOWARD (1918–1992, United States)

Resistance to the disturbance is the disturbance.

—VERNON HOWARD (1918–1992, United States)

Soon the child's clear eye is clouded over by ideas and opinions, preconceptions and abstractions. Simple free being becomes encrusted with the burdensome armor of the ego. Not until years later does an instinct come that a vital sense of mystery has been withdrawn. The sun glints through the pines, and the heart is pierced in a moment of reality and strange pain, like a memory of paradise. After that day . . . we become seekers.

—PETER MATTHIESSEN (1927–, United States)

An individual has not started living until he can rise above the narrow confines of his individualistic concerns to the broader concerns of all humanity.

—MARTIN LUTHER KING JR. (1929–1968, United States)

Most people, even though they don't know it, are asleep. They're born asleep, they live asleep, they marry in their sleep, they breed children in their sleep, they die in their sleep without ever waking up. They never understand the loveliness and the beauty of this thing that we call human existence. You know, all mystics—Catholic, Christian, non-Christian, no matter what their theology, no matter what their religion—are unanimous on one thing: that all is well, all is well. Though everything is a mess, all is well. Strange paradox, to be sure. But, tragically, most people never get to see that all is well because they are asleep. They are having a nightmare.

—ANTHONY DE MELLO (1931–1987, British India)

We are mystical. In other words our roots are in fact religious and artistic, and therefore non-rational, or rather supra-rational. As soon as our material needs are satisfied, deeper needs assert themselves. It is now twenty centuries since Jesus declared that "man does not live by bread alone," and we know today that not even the most effective psychoanalytical treatment can cure us of a deep sense of disquiet within us. There is not a superman or revolutionary who is not beset by unappeased desires. The Fathers of the Christian Church, for whom prayer was as natural as breathing, discovered this truth before we did, saying, "Birds fly, fishes swim, and man prays." Islamic spiritual writers would later express the same idea, saying that the first cry of the new-born babe and the last breath of the dying person together make up and proclaim the divine name.

—JEAN-CLAUDE BARREAU (1933–, France)

May the sun bring you new energy every day.
May the moon softly restore you by night.
May the rain wash away your worries.
May the breeze blow new strength into your being.
May you walk gently through the world and know its beauty all the days of your life.

—APACHE BLESSING

SECTION TWO

THE SEARCH

EVERYBODY'S SEARCHING
FOR SOMETHING

Sweet dreams are made of this . . .
Who am I to disagree?
Travel the world and the seven seas,
Everybody's looking for something.

—THE EURYTHMICS, 1983

I n 1983, an unknown British pop duo topped the U.S. charts with the record *Sweet Dreams (Are Made of This)*. The message in the title song, carried along by a catchy, almost hypnotic melody, hit home; it expressed—in music—the discontent of myriad generations leading up to that time. But its popularity wasn't just because it spoke to this social unrest; there was more to it than just that. The lyrics to this song touched upon a certain celestial law: It isn't just "everybody"—as in you and me—that's searching "the world and the seven seas" for the sweetness of dreams yet to be answered. The truth is that *every living thing is searching for something to fulfill itself*; it is the essence of Great Nature herself to seek out her own highest possibilities. A moment's examination of this important idea reveals a lifetime's worth of invaluable self-knowledge.

Can we see how, in one form or another, everything in creation longs to touch and to be touched? Flowers and trees stretch their leaves and limbs up to the sun, just as it reaches down to touch them. After all, to what end the timeless nature of such radiance, if not to grant life to whatever forms it temporarily animates? Upon examination, we can clearly see that this invisible law of mutual attraction permeates the whole of nature; it is the rule, not the exception.

Fields of grain summon small birds to carry away their seeds; every breeze searches for something to move. Raindrops rush down to slake the thirst of a parched earth, even as water-laden clouds are drawn high into the skies so they can pour themselves out. Streams seek out rivers that rush down to merge with the sea. It's really quite clear: the great circle of life is imbued with this unique kind of "gravity" where all that lives is drawn to join itself to a larger body of life. And, even though unable to do otherwise, we can see how all of nature's creatures work together in this way for a common good: *They seek and serve each other in order to complete and perfect one another in a whole that's greater than the sum of its parts.* This force that draws a bee to pollinate a flower, or a predator to consume its prey, is the touch of Mother Nature's plan; through it, she accounts for the continuing perfection of the almost infinite number of creatures she holds in her hands.

Yet, as beautiful and whole as this system may sound, there's literally a "catch" to the powers needed to maintain such order. While the *forms and functions* of these creatures evolve over time—allowing them to meet the challenges of environmental changes, *their character remains essentially unchanged.* They are without choice when it comes to answering the demands of their nature. The timeless migrations of great beasts, the annual return of fish, birds, or turtles to their place of birth—including the predators called there to await their passage—all of these creatures serve planetary forces that care nothing for their *individual* lives.

This same law of attraction is *always at work within us,* asserting itself upon our lower (animal) nature as well. Its influence goes unrecognized by the sleeping masses but for those "with eyes to see," its manifestations are evident in our globally accepted social conventions.

Though we may have never looked at it in this way before, a fifty-mile-long, four-hundred-foot-wide stream of cars slowly rolling along on a crowded freeway is a kind of daily migration. And what is the universal need to "feather" our nest, dominate a competitor or family member, attract the best sexual partner, make babies or plans to find better "hunting" grounds?

In fact, the hidden nature of almost all that we do on a collective basis is the direct, but unseen, effect of this one great unconscious desire to search out what we believe will complete us, drawing us to seek "greener pastures" by the deft touch of its magnetic hand, but never allowing us to rest. Over countless ages untold billions of us have answered Nature's "call"—much in the same way as a leaf says "yes" to the wind that carries it away. Yet, what do we receive in return for our faithful, if unquestioned consent? We're provided with a fragile, deceptive contentment; our reward is a momentary sense of fulfillment that, in most cases, passes from sight as soon as do the temporary conditions that provided it for us.

Fortunately, for those who seek to discover the truth behind this almost inconsolable discontent, every now and then certain individuals appear who see things as they are. One such revelation is found in Ecclesiastes 2:4–11, written between 250 and 180 BCE, where we share with the writer what we might hear a close friend tell us, privately, over a cup of coffee. From this short piece of Old Testament scripture, we can glean two things at once: first, how little human consciousness has changed over countless years, and second, the inevitable sorrow that comes with having searched for lasting contentment in all the wrong places. The language may be strange to our ear, but its lesson certainly isn't.

I made me great works; I builded me houses; I planted me vineyards: I made me gardens and orchards, and I planted trees in them of all kind of fruits: I got me servants and maidens. I gathered me also silver and gold. So I was great more than all that were before me. And whatsoever mine eyes desired I kept not from them, I withheld not my heart from any joy; for my heart rejoiced in all my labour. Then I looked on all the works that my hands had wrought, and on the labour that I had laboured to do: and, behold, all was vanity and vexation of spirit, and there was no profit under the sun.

Where are we to find a solution to this seemingly inescapable situation, where our best instincts betray us because all they're empowered to do is to sell us a return ticket to the places we just left? Rumi, the 13th-century God-intoxicated Persian poet, tells us that if we wish to bring an end to this cycle of our discontent, then we must "Find the antidote in the venom!" Now let's prove the truth of this counterintuitive prescription.

Whenever we dare to stand in the light of some unwanted truth about how powerless we are to change who or what we've been—where we see that our present choices are secretly a part of what's holding us captive— we're always shown two things at once. First, and perhaps most important: *we see what doesn't work*; we see that our present level of understanding can't lead us to freedom because its desires are a part of what has delivered us into our "prison" of the moment. And the second part of this revelation stands in relief of the first, much like the rising sun reveals a new day. It's quite clear: we know now that if we're to succeed in our search for wholeness, for

Holiness—call it what you will—we not only require a *new and higher order of self-knowledge,* but one that must also take us in *a completely new direction.* Yet, where is one to look when all the known roads through this world lead back to the same level of reality from which we started our journey?

Dr. Maurice Nicoll, noted 20th-century British psychiatrist, author, and spiritual teacher, provides us with an accurate diagnosis of our condition, as well as suggesting the new direction we must take if we wish to bring an end to our constant discontent. He stresses that if we hope to realize the lasting sense of wholeness for which we long, *we must find its secret source within us.*

> *Man has inner necessities; his emotional life is not satisfied by outer things. His organization is not only to be explained in terms of adaptation to outer life. He needs ideas to give meaning to his existence. There is that in him that can grow and develop—some further state of himself—not lying in "tomorrow," but above him.*

Here we glimpse the promise of our own greater possibilities yet unrealized; disclosed is the reason why we can't shake our sense of being incomplete in spite of all we've acquired. After all, what hope is there of finding in the world situated *around us* something that can answer our longing to be whole, to be one with life, *when this need itself comes into us from a world* above *us*? Small wonder we search in vain! It is *a divine discontent* that drives us in our search for someone or something that might grant our restless heart the peace it seeks.

None are immune to the disconcerting touch of this celestial longing. Its invisible presence permeates our being and—under certain circumstances—provides a glimpse of what awaits us, just above our present nature. In such moments we come to understand—by yet another magnitude of brilliance—that what we had once taken to be the sun was nothing more than the light of a waxing moon. But don't be misled; there is nothing disheartening in moments such as these. In fact, the experience is quite the opposite. As we are about to learn, nothing proves the existence of a timeless Love more than coming face-to-face with the clockwork-like machinations of one's own heart.

The great Viennese composer Wolfgang Amadeus Mozart confirms this paradoxical finding. His confession not only provides insight into this grand scale of celestial life, but it also offers us, at once, the promise of discovering these same heights within ourselves.

I have never written the music that was in my heart to write; perhaps I never shall with this brain and these fingers, but I know that hereafter it will be written: when, instead of these few inlets of the senses through which we now secure impressions from all without, there shall be a flood of impressions from all sides; and instead of these few tones of our little octave there shall be an infinite score of harmonies—for I feel it, I am sure of it. This world of music, whose borders even now I have scarcely entered, is a reality, is immortal.

—CHARLES PATTERSON, *The Rhythm of Life*

In the section that follows, you will share in the accounts and discoveries of many individuals who, just like you, set out to find new, true answers that could stand up to the test of passing time with its ever-changing conditions. Welcome these inward and uplifting thoughts as if they were your own, for in one sense . . . they are. Take them into your heart; search out their hidden meaning. Answer their clarion call. If you will, you can't help but rise into the world from which they have come.

THE MASTERS SPEAK OF THE SEARCH

There's more to the truth than just the facts.

—AUTHOR UNKNOWN

To do rightly by the cosmos depends on timing: right doing, right being at the right time and place. This right guidance, found in every heart, finds its source in the universal Heart. This rightness is ultimate good, ultimate happiness and joy. The joy comes naturally to and through a life lived in moment-by-moment contact with the truth behind all nature, for its own sake and not for anything else.

—ZOROASTRIAN PRAYER (1700–1500 BCE, Persia)

Do not be under the delusion that God is somewhere and you have to search for Him; God is in you.

—ATHARVA VEDA (1200–1000 BCE, India)

God hath framed the mind of man as a mirror of glass,
capable of the image of the universal world, and joyful
to receive the impression thereof, as the eye joyeth to
receive light.

—SOLOMON (ca. 1000 BCE, Jerusalem)

Whoever sees all beings in the soul and the soul in all
beings . . .
What delusion or sorrow is there for one who sees unity?
It has filled all. It is radiant, incorporeal, invulnerable . . .
Wise, intelligent, encompassing, self-existent,
it organizes objects throughout eternity.

—UPANISHADS (800–400 BCE, Pre-Buddhist Era India)

The Way that can be named is not the Way.

—LAO TZU (ca. 570–490 BCE, China)

Whosoever bendeth himself shall be straightened. Whosoever emptieth himself shall be filled. Whosoever weareth
himself away shall be renewed. Whosoever humbleth himself
shall be exalted. Whosoever exalteth himself shall be abased.
Therefore doth the Sage cling to simplicity.

—LAO TZU (ca. 570–490 BCE, China)

Suffering, if it does not diminish love, will transport you to the furthest shore.

—BUDDHA (ca. 565–483 BCE, India)

Surely it is the maxim of loving-kindness: Do not unto others what you would not have done unto you.

—CONFUCIUS (551–479 BCE, China)

One who knows the enemy and knows himself will not be endangered in a hundred engagements. One who does not know the enemy but knows himself will sometimes be victorious, sometimes meet with defeat. One who knows neither the enemy nor himself will invariably be defeated in every engagement.

—SUN-TZU (ca. 500 BCE, China)

Those whose minds are attracted to my invisible nature have a great labor to encounter, because an invisible path is difficult to be found by corporal beings.

—BHAGAVAD GITA (500–200 BCE, India)

This is the sum of duty: Do naught unto others which would cause you pain if done to you.

—MAHABHARATA (400 BCE–200 CE, India)

The perfect man employs his mind as a mirror. It grasps
nothing; it refuses nothing. It receives, but does not keep.

—CHUANG-TZU (369–286 BCE, China)

Let us be silent, for so are the gods.

—ANCIENT SAYING

Easy is the descent into the lower world.
Night and day the door of glowing Dis* stands open.
But to recall thy steps and pass out to the upper air
This is the task, this is the work.

—VIRGIL (70–19 BCE, Gaul)

It is not because things are difficult that we do not dare: it is
because we do not dare that they are difficult.

—SENECA (ca. 3 BCE–65 CE, Rome)

Why does no man confess his vices? Because he is yet in
them; 'tis for a waking man to tell his dream.

—SENECA (ca. 3 BCE–65 CE, Rome)

* God of the underworld.

Bring all opposites inside yourself and reconcile them; understand that you are everywhere, on the land, in the sea, in the sky; realize that you haven't yet been begotten, that you are still in the womb, that you are young, that you are old, that you are dead, that you are in the world beyond the grave; hold all this in your mind, all times and places, all substances and qualities and magnitudes: then you can perceive God.

—HERMETIC WRITINGS
(1st–3rd c. CE, Greece or Egypt)

To live in the light of the universal order is to be awake, to turn aside into our own microcosm is to go to sleep.

—PLUTARCH (45–125, Greece)

All things whatsoever ye would that men should do to you, do ye even so them; for this is the law and the prophets.

—JESUS CHRIST (Quoted in Matthew, New Testament, 55–60)

No one of you is a believer until he desires for his brother that which he desires for himself.

—ISLAMIC SAYING

We are saved by hope; but hope that is seen is not hope: for who hopeth for that which he seeth?

—ROMANS, NEW TESTAMENT (55–56)

There is only one thing for which God sent me into this world and that is to perfect my nature in all sorts of virtue or strength, and there is no thing that I cannot use for that purpose.

—EPICTETUS (55–135, Phrygia, Asia Minor)

The disciples said to him, "Tell us what our end will be." Jesus said, "If you haven't found the beginning, why ask about the end? For where the beginning is, the end is also. Blessed are those who stand at the beginning, for they will know the end, and they will not taste death."

—GOSPEL OF THOMAS (60–140, Egypt)

The kingdom of Heaven is within you, and whosoever knoweth himself shall find it.

—GOSPEL OF THOMAS (60–140, Egypt)

He who has seen present things has seen all, both every-thing which has taken place from all eternity and everything

50 The Seeker, the Search, the Sacred

which will be for time without end; for all things are of one kin and of one form.

—MARCUS AURELIUS (121–180, Rome)

What is hateful to you, do not do to your fellow man. That is the entire Law; all the rest is commentary.

—TALMUD (2nd–5th c.)

If the world goes against truth, then Athanasius goes against the world.

—ATHANASIUS (ca. 295–373, Greece)

Peter of Damascus assures us that "nothing is better than to realize one's weakness and ignorance, and nothing is worse than not to be aware of them."

—PHILOKALIA (4th–15th c., Corinth)

Great endeavors and hard struggles await those who are converted, but afterwards inexpressible joy. If you want to light a fire, you are troubled at first by smoke, and your eyes water. But in the end you achieve your aim. Now it is written: "Our God is a consuming fire." So we must light the divine fire in us with tears and struggle.

—ABBA POEMEN (340–450, Egypt)

He alone knows himself in the best way possible who thinks of himself as being nothing.

—St. John Chrysostom (347–407, Greece)

The mind should be kept independent of any thoughts that arise within it. If the mind depends on anything, it has no sure haven.

—Diamond Sutra (4th c., China)

If you walk toward Him, He comes to you running.

—Muhammad (ca. 570–632, Mecca, Saudi Arabia)

The Almighty created the angels and conferred reason upon them, and He created the beasts and conferred passion upon them, and He created man and conferred reason and passion both upon him. He whose reason prevails over his passion is higher than the angels, and he whose passion prevails over his reason is lower than the beasts.

—Muhammad (ca. 570–632, Mecca, Saudi Arabia)

Glory be to God who has not given to his creatures any way to attain knowledge of him except by means of their helplessness and their hopelessness of ever reaching such attainment.

—ABU BAKR AS-SIDDIQ (573–634, Mecca, Saudi Arabia)

Many are avidly seeking, but they alone find who remain in silence. . . . Those who delight in a multitude of words, even though they say admirable things, are empty within. If you love truth, be a lover of silence. Silence, like the sunlight, will illuminate you in God and will deliver you from the phantoms of ignorance. Silence will unite your soul to God.

—ISAAC OF NINEVEH (unknown–ca. 700, Qatar)

You ask why I make my home in the mountain first, and I smile, and am silent, and even my soul remains quiet: it lives in the other world which no one owns.

—LI-PO (701–762, China)

For thirty years I sought God. But when I looked carefully I found that in reality God was the seeker and I the sought.

—BAYAZID BASTAMI (804–874, Persia)

The more a man enters the light of understanding, the more aware he is of his own ignorance. And when the light reveals itself fully and unites with him and draws him into itself, so

that he finds himself alone in a sea of light, then he is emptied of all knowledge and immersed in absolute unknowing.

—SYMEON THE YOUNGER (ca. 949–1022, Constantinople)

When thou givest to God thy nothingness, He gives to thee
His All.

— ABUL-HASAN AL-KHARQANI (963–1033, Persia)

The true man of God sits in the midst of his fellow-men,
and rises and eats and sleeps and marries and buys and sells
and gives and takes in the bazaars and spends the days with
other people, and yet never forgets God even for a single
moment.

—ABI'L KHAYR (967–1049, Persia)

Bring all of yourself to his door: bring only a part, and you've
brought nothing at all.

—HAKIM SANAI (1080–1131, Persia)

If you seek, how is that different from pursuing sound and
form? If you don't seek, how are you different from earth,
wood, or stone? You must seek without seeking.

—WU-MEN HUIKAI (1183–1260, China)

Always check your inner state
with the lord of your heart.
Copper doesn't know it's copper,
until it's changed to gold.
Your loving doesn't know its majesty,
until it knows its helplessness.

—JALAL AL-DIN RUMI (ca. 1207–1273, Balkh, Persia)

An empty mirror and your worst destructive habits,
when they are held up to each other,
that's when the real making begins.
That's what art and crafting are.
A tailor needs a torn garment to practice his expertise.
The trunks of trees must be cut and cut again
so they can be used for fine carpentry.

—JALAL AL-DIN RUMI (ca. 1207-1273, Balkh, Persia)

To be nothing is the precondition of being.

—JALAL AL-DIN RUMI (ca. 1207–1273, Balkh, Persia)

He who learns the rules of wisdom, without conforming to
them in his life, is like a man who labours in his field, but did
not sow.

—SAADI (ca. 1213–1292, Persia)

Mark how to know yourself. To know himself a man must ever be on the watch over himself, holding his outer faculties. This discipline must be continued until he reaches a state of consciousness. . . . The object is to reach a state of consciousness—a new state of oneself. It is to reach now, where one is present to oneself. "What I say unto you I say unto all, be awake."

—MEISTER ECKHART (1260–ca. 1327, Thuringia)

The shell must be cracked apart if what is in it is to come out, for if you want the kernel you must break the shell. And therefore if you want to discover nature's nakedness, you must destroy its symbols, and the farther you get in the nearer you come to its essence. When you come to the One that gathers all things up into itself, there you must stay.

—MEISTER ECKHART (1260–ca. 1327, Thuringia)

This place where you are right now God circled on a map for you.

—HAFEZ (1315–1390, Persia)

If you wish to grow in your spiritual life, you must not allow yourself to be caught up in the workings of the world; you must find time alone, away from the noise and confusion, away from the allure of power and wealth.

—THOMAS A' KEMPIS (ca. 1380–1471, the Netherlands)

Settle yourself in solitude, and you will come upon Him in yourself.

—ST. TERESA (1515–1582, Spain)

Of all knowledge the wise and good seek most to know themselves.

—WILLIAM SHAKESPEARE (1564–1616, England)

All truths are easy to understand once they are discovered: the point is to discover them.

—GALILEO GALILEI (1564–1642, Italy)

He to whom time is like eternity, and eternity like time, is free.

—JACOB BOEHME (1575–1624, Germany)

We could come into a new reality of our being and perceive everything in a new relation if we can stand still from self-thinking and self-willing and stop the wheel of imagination and the senses.

—JACOB BOEHME (1575–1624, Germany)

He that confesses his sin begins his journey toward salvation; he that is sorry for it mends his pace; he that forsakes it is at his journey's end.

—FRANCIS QUARLES (1592–1644, England)

The highest wisdom consists in this, for man to know himself, because in him God has placed his eternal word.

—ALI PULI (17th c., Mauritania)

The end of all learning is to know God, and out of that knowledge to love and imitate him.

—JOHN MILTON (1608–1674, England)

I know that for the right practice of it (the presence of the Lord) the heart must be empty of all other things, because God will possess the heart *alone*; and as He cannot possess it *alone* without emptying it of all besides, so neither can he act *there*, and do in it what he pleases, unless it be left vacant to him.

—BROTHER LAWRENCE (1611–1691, France)

Let us put the ideas of our mind, just as we put things of the laboratory, to the test of experience.

—JOHN LOCKE (1632–1704, England)

If I have ever made any valuable discoveries, it has been owing more to patient attention, than to any other talent.

—SIR ISAAC NEWTON (1642–1727, England)

Weakness is very painful, but also very useful. While any self-love remains, you are afraid that it will be discovered. As long as the least bit of self-love remains in the secret parts of your heart, God will hunt it down, and, by some infinitely merciful blow, force your selfishness and jealousy out of hiding. The poison then becomes the cure. Self-love, exposed to the light, sees itself in horror. The flattering lifelong illusions you have held of your self are forced to die. God lets you see who you really worship: yourself.

—FRANÇOIS FENELON (1651–1715, France)

The greatest of all crosses is self. If we die in part every day, we shall have but little to do on the last. These little daily deaths will destroy the power of the final dying.

—FRANÇOIS FENELON (1651–1715, France)

But what is the secret of finding this treasure? There isn't one. This treasure is everywhere . . . God's activity runs through the universe. It wells up around and penetrates every created being. Where they are, there it is also. It goes ahead of them, it is with them, and it follows them. All they have to do is let its waves sweep them onward, fulfill the simple duties of their religion and state, cheerfully accept all the troubles they meet, and submit to God's will in all they have to do. This is true spirituality, which is valid for all times and for everyone. We cannot become truly good in a better, more marvelous, and yet easier way than by the simple use of the means offered us by God: the ready acceptance of all that comes to us at each moment of our lives.

—JEAN PIERRE DE CAUSSADE (1675–1761, France)

You can have no greater sign of a confirmed pride than when you think you are humble enough.

—WILLIAM LAW (1686–1761, England)

The path of sorrow, and that path alone, leads to the land where sorrow is unknown; no traveler ever reached that blessed abode who found not thorns and briars in his road.

—WILLIAM COWPER (1731–1768, England)

"Die and become," that is, "Die to this existence and be reborn on a higher level."

—JOHANN WOLFGANG VON GOETHE (1749–1832, Germany)

In this patient, though uncheered, obedience, we become prepared for light. The soul gathers force.

—WILLIAM ELLERY CHANNING (1780–1842, United States)

Weak eyes are fondest of glittering objects.

—THOMAS CARLYLE (1795–1881, Scotland)

Welcome evermore to gods and men is the self-helping man. For him all doors are flung wide: him all tongues greet, all honors crown, all eyes follow with desire. Our love goes out to him and embraces him, because he did not need it. We solicitously and apologetically caress and celebrate him, because he held on his way and scorned our disapprobation.

The gods love him because men hated him. "To the persevering mortal," said Zoroaster, "the blessed Immortals are swift."

—RALPH WALDO EMERSON (1803–1882, United States)

So, in regard to disagreeable and formidable things, prudence does not consist in evasion or flight, but in courage. He who wishes to walk in the most peaceful parts of life with any serenity must screw himself up to resolution. Let him front the object of his worst apprehension, and his stoutness will commonly make his fear groundless.

—RALPH WALDO EMERSON (1803–1882, United States)

I have been driven many times to my knees by the overwhelming conviction that I had nowhere else to go. My own wisdom, and that of all about me, seemed insufficient for the day.

—ABRAHAM LINCOLN (1809–1865, United States)

When you travel to the Celestial City, carry no letters of introduction. When you knock, ask to see God, none of the servants.

—HENRY DAVID THOREAU (1817–1862, United States)

The frontiers are not east or west, north or south but wherever a man fronts a fact.

—HENRY DAVID THOREAU (1817–1862, United States)

Humility like darkness reveals the heavenly lights.

—HENRY DAVID THOREAU (1817–1862, United States)

The whole history of the progress of human liberty shows that all concessions yet made to her august claims, have been born of earnest struggle. Those who profess to favor freedom and yet depreciate agitation, are men who want crops without plowing up the ground, they want rain without thunder and lightning. They want the ocean without the awful roar of its many waters.

—FREDERICK DOUGLASS (1818–1895, United States)

O Lord, I cannot plead my love of thee:
I plead thy love of me;
The shallow conduit hails the unfathomed sea.

—CHRISTINA ROSSETTI (1830–1894, England)

I am not afraid of storms, for I am learning how to sail my ship.

—LOUISA MAY ALCOTT (1832–1888, United States)

For whilst in one sense we give up self to live the universal and absolute life of reason, yet that to which we thus surrender ourselves is in reality our truer self. The life of absolute truth or reason is not a life that is foreign to us. If it is above us, it is also within us. In yielding to it we are not submitting to an outward and arbitrary law or to an external authority, but to a law which has become our own law, an authority which has become enthroned in the inmost essence of our being.

—EDWARD CAIRD (1835–1908, Scotland)

Everyone foolishly assumes that his clock alone tells correct time. Christians claim to possess exclusive truth. . . . Countless varieties of Hindus insist that their sect, no matter how small and insignificant, expresses the ultimate position. Devout Muslims maintain that Koranic revelation supersedes all others. The entire world is being driven insane by this single phrase: "My religion alone is true." O Mother, you have shown me that no clock is entirely accurate. Only the transcendent sun of knowledge remains on time. Who can make a system from Divine Mystery? But if any sincere practitioner, within whatever culture or religion, prays and meditates with great devotion and commitment to Truth alone, Your Grace will flood his mind and heart, O Mother. His particular sacred tradition will be opened and illuminated. He will reach the one goal of spiritual evolution.

—RAMAKRISHNA (1836–1886, India)

But where can man find the truth? If he seeks deep enough in himself, he will find it revealed, each man may know his own heart. He may send a ray of his intelligence into the depths of his soul and search its bottom; he may find it to be as infinitely deep as the sky above his head. He may find corals and pearls, or watch the monsters of the deep. If his thought is steady and unwavering, he may enter the innermost sanctuary of his own temple and see the goddess unveiled. Not everyone can penetrate into such depths, because the thought is easily led astray; but the strong and persistent searcher will penetrate veil after veil, until at the innermost center he discovers the germ of truth, which, awakened to consciousness, will grow into a sun that illuminates the whole of the interior world, wherein everything is contained.

—FRANZ HARTMANN (1838–1912, Germany)

Many of life's failures are people who did not realize how close they were to success when they gave up.

—THOMAS EDISON (1847–1931, United States)

If a man would find the Key of Knowledge, let him find himself.

—JAMES ALLEN (1864–1912, England)

Oh, thou that pinest in the imprisonment of the Actual, and criest bitterly to the gods for a kingdom wherein to rule and create, know this of a truth: the thing thou seekest is already within thee, here and now, couldest thou only see!

—JAMES ALLEN (1864–1912, England)

I have found by experience that man makes his plans to be often upset by God, but, at the same time, where the ultimate goal is the search of truth, no matter how a man's plans are frustrated the issue is never injurious and often better than anticipated.

—MOHANDAS GANDHI (1869–1948, British India)

One does not discover new lands without consenting to lose sight of the shore for a very long time.

—ANDRÉ GIDE (1869–1951, France)

Such is the nature of man,
that for your first gift—he prostrates himself;
for your second—kisses your hand;
for the third—fawns;
for the fourth—just nods his head once;
for the fifth—becomes too familiar;

for the sixth—insults you;
and for the seventh—sues you because he was not
given enough.

     —George Gurdjieff (ca. 1872–1949, Caucasus region)

The quarrels of religious sects are like the disputing of pots,
which shall be alone allowed to hold the immortalising nec-
tar. Let them dispute, but the thing for us is to get at the nec-
tar in whatever pot and attain immortality.

     —Sri Aurobindo (1872–1950, Calcutta, India)

The observer, when he seems to himself to be observing a
stone, is really, if physics is to be believed, observing the
effects of the stone upon himself.

     —Bertrand Russell (1872–1970, England)

Men stumble over the truth from time to time, but most pick
themselves up and hurry off as if nothing had happened.

     —Winston Churchill (1874–1965, England)

Do not be bewildered by the surfaces: in the depths all
becomes law.

     —Rainer Maria Rilke (1875–1926, Bohemia)

There is no coming to consciousness without pain.

—CARL JUNG (1875–1961, Switzerland)

It is not necessary to go off on a tour of great cathedrals in order to find the Deity. Look within. You have to sit still to do it.

—ALBERT SCHWEITZER (1875–1965, Germany)

Systems and schools can indicate methods and ways, but no system or school whatever can do for a man the work that he must do himself. Inner growth, a change of being, depend entirely upon the work which a man must do on himself.

—P. D. OUSPENSKY (1878–1947, Russia)

Another thing that people must sacrifice is their suffering. It is very difficult also to sacrifice one's suffering. A man will renounce any pleasures you like, but he will not give up his suffering. Man is made in such a way that he is never so much attached to anything as he is to his suffering. And it is necessary to be free from suffering. No one who is not free from suffering, who has not sacrificed his suffering, can work. Later on a great deal must be said about suffering. Nothing can be attained without suffering, but at the same time one must begin by sacrificing suffering. Now, decipher what this means.

—P. D. OUSPENSKY (1878–1947, Russia)

The degree of freedom from unwanted thoughts and the degree of concentration on a single thought are the measures to gauge spiritual progress.

—RAMANA MAHARSHI (1879–1950, Tiruchuzhi, Tamil Nadu)

Truth is not something lying in time, in the future, but is something here, now, only above us, above our present consciousness.

—MAURICE NICOLL (1884–1953, Scotland)

If we could penetrate to the eternal reality of our own being, we would find the one and only solution for every situation— in the right sense of our own existence, primarily in itself.

—MAURICE NICOLL (1884–1953, Scotland)

Never mistake knowledge for wisdom. One helps you make a living, the other helps you make a life.

—ELEANOR ROOSEVELT (1884–1962, United States)

There is in me something mysterious that nothing is able to grasp, something that no thought or feeling can help me know. It appears only when I am not caught in the web of my thoughts and emotions. It is the unknown, which cannot be grasped with what I know.

—JEANNE MATIGNON DE SALZMANN
(1889–1990, Switzerland)

True education is to learn how to think, not what to think. If you know how to think, if you really have that capacity, then you are a free human being—free of dogmas, superstitions, ceremonies—and therefore you can find out what religion is.

—J. KRISHNAMURTI (1895–1986, India)

I tell thee, doubt is as a precious ointment;
Though it burns, it shall heal greatly.

—J. KRISHNAMURTI (1895–1986, India)

The test of a first-rate intelligence is the ability to hold two opposed ideas in the same mind at the same time.

—F. SCOTT FITZGERALD (1896–1940, United States)

The moment we make up our mind, that we are going on with this determination to exact God over all, we step out of the world's parade. We shall find ourself out of adjustment to the ways of the world, and increasingly so as we make progress in The Holy Way. We shall acquire a new viewpoint; a new and different psychology will be formed within us; a new power will begin to surprise us by its upsurging and its outgoing.

—A. W. TOZER (1897–1963, United States)

There are two basic duties for man in this life; one is to serve nature and the other is to find God.

—J. G. BENNETT (1897–1974, England)

As he advances in the idea of being detached from results and possessions, he will inevitably have to advance in the idea of being detached from concern about his own spiritual development. If he is to relinquish the ego, he will also have to relinquish his attempts to improve it. This applies just as much to its character as to its ideas.

—PAUL BRUNTON (1898–1981, England)

Even if our efforts of attention seem for years to be producing no result, one day a light that is in exact proportion to them will flood the soul.

—SIMONE WEIL (1909–1943, France)

Very well, then: why are you attached to any one book, or to the words and ways of one saint when he himself tells you to let them go and walk in simplicity? To hang on to him as if to make a method of him is to contradict him and to go in the opposite direction to the one in which he would have you travel.

—THOMAS MERTON (1915–1968, France)

In humility is the greatest freedom. As long as you have to defend the imaginary self that you think is important, you lose your peace of heart. As soon as you compare that shadow with the shadows of other people, you lose all joy, because you have begun to trade in unrealities, and there is no joy in things that do not exist.

—THOMAS MERTON (1915–1968, France)

Steadily he approaches the point where what is unknown is not a mere blank space in a web of words but a window in the mind, a window whose name is not ignorance but wonder.

—ALAN WATTS (1915–1973, England)

When you choose the truth, truth chooses you.

—VERNON HOWARD (1918–1992, United States)

Your humiliation is your salvation.

—VERNON HOWARD (1918–1992, United States)

The only way to avoid death is not to be born in the first place. In death there is union with the Beloved. The real skill is to reach the secret of death before dying.

—JOHN ALGEO (1930–, United States)

Silence is not the absence of sound, but the absence of self.

—ANTHONY DE MELLO (1931–1987, British India)

When the heart weeps because it has lost, the spirit laughs because it has found.

—SUFI SAYING

Arjuna is the ascending human soul. Krishna is the descending divine Soul. Finally they meet. The human soul says to the divine Soul: "I need you." The divine Soul says to the human soul: "I need you, too. I need you for my self-manifestation. You need me for your self-realisation." Arjuna says: "O, Krishna, you are mine, absolutely mine." Krishna says: "O, Arjuna, no mine, no thine. We are the Oneness complete, within, without."

> —SRI CHINMOY GHOSE, COMMENTARY ON THE BHAGAVAD
> GITA (1931–2007, British India)

If you think you're free, there's no escape possible.

> —RAM DASS (1931–, United States)

So here we are, explorers in a vast universe at the end of the first decade of the third millennium. We've peered back to the dawn of time to question the Big Bang. We have learned to take our baby steps into space. But the thing we desire most continues to elude us. The inner path of Peace and its twin, the outer path of Justice, are difficult to find in a world confronted with war, political and economic terrorism and injustice. To seek inner peace and use it publically at this time in the search for outer peace is our greatest challenge.

> —DR. J. J. HURTAK (1940–, United States)

SECTION THREE

THE SACRED

AS ABOVE, SO BELOW

F or many months now there had been no peace in the forest. What started as a simple difference of opinion between former friends, a gray tree squirrel and a red fox who lived in the same section of the woods, had escalated into a full-scale conflict involving all the animals for miles around.

It seems the whole thing began when the squirrel told the fox that of all the creatures, he was by far the happiest of the lot. "Not a chance," fired back the red fox. "I am the happiest of all!" After a brief skirmish over bragging rights, with no clear victor, the irritated fox went on to mention the dispute to one of his friends, a skunk that lived in the hollow log just above his den.

Of course, the skunk took great offense at the whole idea that the fox could possibly be happier than he, and soon they too were embroiled in a dispute that caught the attention of a scrub jay and a woodpecker who just happened to be overhead.

A moment later, all four of them were arguing over who was the happiest of all, and, just like a wildfire, the conflict spread out from there. Less than two weeks later, there wasn't a single creature left in the woods that wasn't involved in the challenge as to who should wear the mantle of "most happy!" Well, that is . . . except for one.

Solomon, the wise old owl of the woods, had no interest in these childish arguments that sometimes broke out among his neighbors and friends. But as the longtime caretaker for all the forest creatures in that region, it was his responsibility to settle these matters as quickly as possible. Besides, he already knew the happiest of all the creatures in the woods; it just happened to be an old friend of his. And so, as he had done many times before, Solomon called for everyone far and wide to attend a special peace council to settle the matter once and for all.

Everyone showed up at the appointed time and place, but the tension was palpable. Of course the crows were carrying on, cawing to be heard above the squawking jays, and joining in the noisy fray were all the other forest dwellers—bears, skunks, bobcats, squirrels, raccoons, and birds of all kinds—each one claiming to be the happiest of all.

Choosing his moment, Solomon stepped into the midst of them and spoke. "Please, my friends, if I may have your attention . . ."

Then, slowly turning his handsomely feathered head in a complete circle to ensure that everyone there knew he was addressing them directly, he continued, "I'm afraid that none of you here today are what you claim to be—"

He barely finished his opening statement before a rumble of troubled mumbles tore through the crowd of would-be winners. A moment later, one of the crows cried out what everyone there was thinking:

"You've got to be kidding! What do you mean *none* of us . . . ? Certainly *one* of us is happiest of all?"

His question wasn't as much directed at Solomon, as it was to win the approval of the crowd whose chorus of supportive voices chimed in almost immediately:

"Yeah, right on!"

"Let the crow speak!"

"It's gotta be one of us!"

"True enough," said Solomon, waiting for them to settle down. "But," he continued, "The happiest one of you isn't even here with us today."

A strained silence fell over the whole gathering, only to be broken by the vicious comment of some creature hiding behind a tree. "Ha! Whoever it is must be a real coward; doesn't even have the guts to show up and claim his prize!"

"Perhaps," said Solomon, carefully measuring his words. "But, then again, this creature—a close friend of mine—never claimed to be anything special in the first place, as all of you have done. So . . . ," and he arched his eyebrows just enough to accentuate the irony of what he would say next, "It seems my friend has no reason to defend himself, let alone contend over a silly title he couldn't care less about."

The certainty with which Solomon spoke, and the obvious truth in his assertion, set off yet another round of grumbles through the crowd. Then a shout rose above all these complaining voices; it sounded more like a demand than a question:

"Tell us, then—if it's none of us here today, who do *you* say is the happiest of us all?"

Solomon paused, took a deep breath, and spoke. "You all know him," he said. "It's Abraham, the old tortoise of the East Glen."

"What!" screamed one of the crows, nearly leaping off its roost in a nearby tree. "You've got to be kidding!" Then the sarcasm in his voice took on a challenging tone. "Come on, man . . . what could Abraham possibly have that we don't?"

With a quick tilt of his head and a small, wry smile, Solomon answered. "What makes Abraham happier than the rest of you all is really quite simple, which is why, I suppose, none of you are able to see it."

"See *what*?" shouted the crow.

"Yes, get on with it!" shouted some of the others.

"Think of it," said Solomon, unthreatened and in no hurry to finish his thought.

"No matter the wild places his journey takes him— regardless of the weather or whatever challenges he may encounter along the way, Abraham's home is always with him."

৵৵

This short story is much more than just a simple meta-phor with spiritual overtones. More often than not, much of what we see in nature stirs in us a sense of something long forgotten. In this instance—as represented by the tortoise whose home is always with him wherever he goes—we're reminded of one of our deepest spiritual longings: to be able to face, without fear, whatever trouble comes our way because the strength we need to do so—wherever we go—*is already a part of who we are.*

Let's look at another example. One reason many of us find ourselves so fascinated with how the branch-bound caterpillar is transformed into an airborne butterfly is that we hope for a similar transfiguration of our own baggage-bound character. We long to rise above our earthly cares. Mother Nature is full of this kind of "magic," inspiring us to wonder about our own latent possibilities. With every act of creation we behold, she beckons to us: "Wake up! An unrealized greatness waits within you! See how the celestial is hidden in the common, and then use this understanding to make your way back to its sacred shore."

Consider for a moment a single oak tree. Every year, throughout its life, it will throw thousands of acorns of measurably different shapes, sizes, and coloration. And hidden within each of these seeds is its possibility to become an oak every bit as grand and spreading as the one from which it originally sprang. So, in a very real sense, each of these little acorns is a great oak; its temporary seed form is but one of the many stages through which it will pass in the timeless life cycle of that species.

Seen this way, the purpose of the acorn doesn't end by "growing up" into a tree. Rather, we can see that *its journey has no beginning and no end*. The acorn that becomes an oak is actually the "prodigal seed," endlessly returning from where it started, reborn again and again as the "lowly" acorn.

The acorn's unique destiny is the same as the tree from which it comes: to continue perfecting the totality of its nature and, in turn, Mother Nature herself. From this new perspective, we can see this seed, its sprouting, and the tree it becomes as they are in *a higher order of reality*: a single nature that expresses itself in three stages of life. These phases appear to be separate to us, but they are not; we are blind to their secret wholeness due to the limitations of our physical senses that are unable to witness their passage through time.

Observing life as we do through our time-based consciousness, our senses are able to see only its individual parts but cannot discern the greater whole from out of which they appear. William Blake, the brilliant 18th-century English poet, confirms this observation:

Shame is Pride's cloak. Prisons are built with stones of law, brothels with bricks of religion. The pride of the peacock is the glory of God. The lust of the goat is the bounty of God. The wrath of the lion is the wisdom of God. The nakedness of woman is the work of God. Excess of sorrow laughs. Excess of joy weeps. The roaring of lions, the howling of wolves, the

raging of the stormy sea, and the destructive sword, are por-
tions of eternity, too great for the eye of man.

—*The Marriage of Heaven and Hell*

Yet, this present set of limitations need not serve as a prison cell for our possibilities, any more than the hard-ened shell of an acorn prevents a tree from growing up and out of it. For within us dwells a divine intelligence whose timeless presence and power—once realized—make good on the promise found in the Gospel of Thomas: "Jesus said: Recognize what is right in front of you, and that which is hidden from you will be revealed to you. Nothing hidden will fail to be displayed." And we find the same idea in the New Testament, Luke 8:17: "For nothing is secret, that shall not be made manifest; neither any-thing hid, that shall not be known."

What is this power that can show us the truth behind the mystery of who and what we are—even as it gives us everything we need to know? A few examples from the history of human discovery prove helpful in our inquiry.

In their time, the Wright brothers watched birds sail through the open skies and "asked" nature if she would divulge to them the principles of flight. As a result of their creative inquiry, today we can fly around the world in a matter of hours.

Albert Einstein, long considered the father of modern physics, "requested" that the universe reveal to him the secret relationship between matter and energy, and the general theory of relativity was born. From this fruit came the seed of other new scientific disciplines, including seminal discoveries leading up to the peacetime use of atomic energy, superconductivity, and gravitational studies that have helped us explore and comprehend the workings hidden in the deepest regions of our universe.

The evidence is indisputable: the mind that wants to know the truth of something, and that's willing to do the work required for such a discovery, will inevitably find that for which it is searching; our highest aspirations are reflections of unrealized possibilities. All scripture, from the East to the West, confirms this timeless truth (*We need only ask, and it shall be given.*)

But the real question before us isn't *how* these individuals came to make their discoveries. We already know that the birth of all things great and true requires discipline, patience, and sacrifice. Rather, what we wish to know is *where* did they find this elevated understanding? In what place are we to seek and search for the timeless laws that alone reveal, and then release us from, our former limitations? The answer is surprising at first glance, but ultimately the most freeing discovery one can make: within each and every one of us already dwells everything that will ever be known; all powers, all possibilities, are a part of our own sacred birthright. This passage from the book of Ecclesiastes adds an important dimension to this idea: "What has been will be again, what has been done will be done again; there is nothing new under the sun."

At first, it may be difficult to even imagine such an idea—that *within us already dwells all that will ever be*. But we mustn't ignore this possibility. We've observed that within the acorn already dwells the mighty oak, and the butterfly *is* the caterpillar from which it emerges. The implication of these discoveries is staggering, and the promise hidden within them, even greater! So let's look at a common life situation—something we've all gone through—to shed more light on these last ideas.

All of us know what it's like to be dogged by parts of us that want to drag us down. Call it what you will: some compulsion or obsession seems to follow us into all our relationships, only to wreck them in one way or another. We struggle as best we can to free ourselves from these dark states but invariably find ourselves short of the mark. Slowly but surely, one thing becomes clear: we start to see that calling upon who and what we have been to save us from our suffering is like asking a windstorm to neatly pile our autumn leaves. So, without giving up, we begin to open our eyes to the truth of our condition, and somewhere in the midst of our misery, we suddenly see our lives in a new kind of light. In this new awareness, a whole new order of self-understanding dawns; and, as it does, our old dark sense of self departs, taking its suffering along with it.

In these healing moments, where we seem to awaken from a bad dream, there comes a new understanding of something we've always known *but had somehow forgotten!* Revelations like these can mean only one thing: all that we need to know to grow beyond who we currently are *is already a part of our true nature.* English poet and playwright, T.S. Eliot, summarizes this idea for us:

> *We shall not cease from exploration, and the end of all our exploring will be to arrive where we started, and know the place for the first time.*

In the first two sections of this book, we learned that in spite of the many differences that seem to exist between peoples the world over—regardless of culture, tradition, environment, or heredity—there is but one seeker, one search, and one sacred object of our desire. We now approach the greatest mystery of all, which the next section intends to illuminate beyond any shadow of doubt.

The celestial source of this sacred being doesn't just live within us; *we are, in fact, one with it.* Our true self is as much a part of its everlasting light as the rays of the setting sun are one with the ocean upon which they dance in delight.

THE MASTERS
SPEAK OF THE SACRED

I sit next to him who remembers me.

—MOSES (PROPHET MUSA) (1526–1406 BCE, Egypt)

I love them that love me; and those that seek me early shall find me.

—PROVERBS, OLD TESTAMENT (ca. 1000–700 BCE)

That thou art.

—UPANISHADS (800–400 BCE, Pre-Buddhist Era India)

Thou dost keep him in perfect peace, whose mind is stayed on thee.

—ISAIAH, OLD TESTAMENT (ca. 700 BCE)

I will give you one heart and a new spirit; I will take from you
your hearts of stone and give you tender hearts of love for God.

—EZEKIEL, OLD TESTAMENT (593–565 BCE)

By the accident of good fortune a man may rule the world for
a time. But by virtue of love he may rule the world forever.

—LAO TZU (ca. 570–490 BCE, China)

When I attained Absolute Perfect Enlightenment, I attained
absolutely nothing. That is why it is called Absolute Perfect
Enlightenment.

—BUDDHA (ca. 565–483 BCE, India)

To those who awake, there is one world in common, but to those
who are asleep, each is withdrawn to a private world of his own.

—HERACLITUS (535–475 BCE, Ephesus, Asia Minor)

There never was a time when I did not exist, nor you, nor
any of these kings. Nor is there any future in which we shall
cease to be.

—BHAGAVAD GITA (500–200 BCE, India)

Light is the shadow of God.

—PLATO (427–347 BCE, Greece)

That which hath been is now; and that which is to be hath already been.

—ECCLESIASTES, OLD TESTAMENT (ca. 250 BCE)

No eye has seen, no ear has heard, no mind has conceived what God has prepared for those who love him.

—ST. PAUL, NEW TESTAMENT (ca. 54, Asia Minor)

Jesus said, "I am the light that is over all things. I am all: from me all came forth, and to me all attained. Split a piece of wood; I am there. Lift up the stone, and you will find me there."

—GOSPEL OF THOMAS (60–140, Egypt)

God is love and he who abides in love abides in God, and God abides in him.

—ST. JOHN, NEW TESTAMENT (ca. 90)

Humanity was free from the beginning. For God is freedom and humanity was made in the image of God.

—IRENAEUS OF LYONS (ca. 115–unknown,
Gaul, Roman Empire)

The highest wisdom consists in this, for man to know himself, because in him God has placed his eternal word.

—THE GOSPEL OF Q (130–250, place unknown)

There is a divine sense higher than human sense, that enables those of pure heart to see God.

—ORIGEN (185–254, Egypt)

Sharing in the divine fullness is such that it makes whoever achieves it ever greater, more illimitable, so as never to cease growing. Because the spring of all reality flows ceaselessly, the being of anyone who shares in it is increased in grandeur by all that springs up within, so that the capacity for receiving grows along with the abundance of good gifts received.

—GREGORY OF NYSSA (335–ca. 394, Caesarea, Cappadocia)

Know to what extent the Creator has honored you above all the rest of creation. The sky is not an image of God, nor is the moon, nor the sun, nor the beauty of the stars, nor anything of what can be seen in creation. You alone have been made the image of the Reality that transcends all understanding, the likeness of imperishable beauty, the imprint of true divinity, the recipient of beatitude, the seal of the true light. When you turn to him you become that which he is himself. . . .

—GREGORY OF NYSSA (335–ca. 394, Caesarea, Cappadocia)

Three brothers were in the habit of going to see the blessed Anthony every year. The first two would ask him questions about their thoughts and the salvation of the soul. But the third would keep silence without asking anything. Eventually Abba Anthony said to him, "You have been coming here to see me for a long time now and you never ask me any questions." The other replied, "One thing is enough for me, Father, to see you."

—ABBA POEMEN (340–450, Egypt)

All of us who are human beings are in the image of God. But to be in his likeness belongs only to those who by great love have attached their freedom to God.

—DIADOCHUS OF PHOTIKE (5th ca., Greece)

I who cannot be fit into universes upon universes, fit into the heart of the sincere believer.

—MUHAMMAD (ca. 570–632, Mecca, Saudi Arabia)

Whoever knows himself knows God.

—MUHAMMAD (ca. 570–632, Mecca, Saudi Arabia)

Only love overcomes the fragmentation of human nature.

—MAXIMUS THE CONFESSOR (580–641, Constantinople)

Allah possesses a drink which is reserved for his intimate friends: when they drink they become intoxicated, when they become intoxicated they become joyful, when they become joyful they become sweet, when they become sweet they begin to melt, when they begin to melt they become free, when they become free they seek, when they seek they find, when they find they arrive, when they arrive they join, and when they join, there is no difference between them and their Beloved.

—ALI IBN ABU TALIB (596–661, Mecca, Saudi Arabia)

When God sees that in all purity of heart you are trusting in him more than in yourself . . . then a strength unknown to you will come to make its dwelling in you. And you will feel in all your senses the power of him who is with you.

—ISAAC OF NINEVEH (unknown–ca. 700, Qatar)

A mind that is truly free has reached the state in which opposites are seen as empty. This is the only freedom.

—HUI-HAI (730–800, China)

So God Most High has said, "When I love a servant, I am his ear, so that he hears by me; I am his eye, so that he sees by me; and I am his tongue, so that he speaks by me."

—DHU'L-NUN AL-MISRI (791–860, Upper Egypt)

When a man can let his heart die, then the primordial spirit wakes to life.

—LU YEN (ca. 800, China)

I made four mistakes in my preliminary steps in this way: I thought that I remember him, that I know Him, that I love Him, and that I seek him, but when I reached Him, I saw that His remembering of me preceded my remembrance of him, that His knowledge about me preceded my knowledge of him, that his love towards me was more ancient than my love towards him, and that he sought me in order that I would begin to seek him.

—BAYAZID BASTAMI (804–874, Persia)

The nature of rain is the same, but it makes thorns grow in the marshes and flowers in the gardens.

—ARABIC SAYING

Again I saw Him in my house. Among all those everyday things He appeared unexpectedly and became unutterably united and merged with me, and leaped over to me without anything in between, as fire to iron, as the light to glass. And He made me like fire and like light. And I became that which I saw before and beheld from afar. I do not know how to relate this miracle to you. And I could not understand and even now I do not entirely understand how He entered into me and how He was united with me. But now that I am united with Him, how can I tell you who He is, who has united with me and with whom I, in turn, am united? I fear that if I related it to you, you would not believe it and, falling from ignorance into blasphemy, my brother, you might lose your soul. He, with whom I am united, and I have become one. But how shall I call myself who was united with Him? God, who is twofold in nature and one in essence, made me also twofold, and endowed me with a twofold name. This is the distinction: I am man by nature, and God by the grace of God.

—SYMEON THE YOUNGER (ca. 949–1022, Constantinople)

Love's conqueror is he whom love conquers.

—HAKIM SANAI (1080–1131, Persia)

While reason is still tracking down the secret, you end your quest on the open field of love.

—HAKIM SANAI (1080–1131, Persia)

An individual drop can be merged with the ocean, and still remain meaningful. He has found his "place."

—FARIDUDDIN ATTAR (ca. 1142–ca. 1220, Nishapur, Khorasan)

One went to the door of the Beloved and knocked.
A voice asked, "Who is there?"
He answered, "It is I."
The voice said, "There is no room for Me and Thee."
The door was shut.
After a year of solitude and deprivation he returned and knocked.
A voice from within asked, "Who is there?"
The man said, "It is Thee."
The door was opened for him.

—JALAL AL-DIN RUMI (ca. 1207–1273, Balkh, Persia)

When the ocean surges,
don't let me just hear it.
Let it splash inside my chest!

—JALAL AL-DIN RUMI (ca. 1207–1273, Balkh, Persia)

Nothing in all creation is so like God as stillness.

—MEISTER ECKHART (1260–ca. 1327, Thuringia)

The eye with which I see God is the same eye with which
God sees me.

—MEISTER ECKHART (1260–ca. 1327, Thuringia)

Thus I was taught that love is our lord's meaning. And I saw
most surely in this and in all, that before God made us he
loved us, which love was never slaked nor ever shall be. And
in this love he has done all his works, and in this love he has
made all things profitable to us, and in this love our life is
everlasting. In our creation we had beginning, but the love
in which he made us was in him from without beginning. In
this love we have our beginning, and all this shall we see in
God without end.

—JULIAN OF NORWICH (1342–ca. 1416, England)

I never think upon eternity without receiving great comfort.
For I say to myself: how could my soul grasp the idea of ever-
lastingness, if the two were not related in some way?

—ST. FRANCIS DE SALES (1567–1622, France)

When thou art gone forth wholly from the creature, and from that which is visible, and art become nothing to all that is nature and creature, then thou art in that Eternal One which is God himself: And then thou shalt perceive and feel in thy interior the highest virtue of love. . . . Whosoever finds it, finds all things.

—JACOB BOEHME (1575–1624, Germany)

It is not "man" in the abstract who recognizes anything. It is always a certain principle, having become active in him, that recognizes its own counterpart in external nature, when it comes in contact with it. Only he in whom is light can see the light; only the element of love can feel love; only the divinity in man can know God in and through man.

—JACOB BOEHME (1575–1624, Germany)

The river has become one with the sea. No, the river does not have all the qualities of the sea, but it is, nonetheless, in the sea.

—JEANNE GUYON (1648–1717, France)

God never ceases to speak to us; but the noise of the world without, and the tumult of our passions within, bewilder us, and prevent us from listening. All must be silent around us, and all must be still within us, when we would listen with our whole souls to this voice. It is a still, small voice, and is only heard by those who listen to no other. Alas! How seldom is it that the soul is so still that it can hear when God speaks to it!

—FRANÇOIS FENELON (1651–1715, France)

The boundless sea has absorbed the river and its limited waters. Now the river shares in all that the sea has. The sea carries the river along; the river cannot carry itself along. Where there is plenty of light there is strong shadow.

—JOHANN WOLFGANG VON GOETHE
(1749–1832, Germany)

Oh how the spell before my sight brings nature's hidden ways to light. See! All things with each other blending, each to each its being lending, all on each in turn depending, heavenly ministers descending, and again to heaven ascending, floating, mingling, interweaving. . . . Can heart of man embrace Illimitable Nature?

—JOHANN WOLFGANG VON GOETHE
(1749–1832, Germany)

To see a world in a grain of sand
And a Heaven in a wild flower
Hold Infinity in the palm of your hand
And Eternity in an hour.

—WILLIAM BLAKE (1757–1827, England)

Our birth is but a sleep and a forgetting.
The soul that rises with us, our life's star,
Hath had elsewhere its setting.
And cometh from afar;
Not in entire forgetfulness,
And not in utter nakedness,
But trailing clouds of glory do we come
From God, who is our home.

—WILLIAM WORDSWORTH (1770–1850, England)

The eternal stars shine out as soon as it is dark enough.

—THOMAS CARLYLE (1795–1881, Scotland)

A little consideration of what takes place around us every
day would show us that a higher law than that of our will
regulates events; that our painful labors are unnecessary, and

fruitless; that only in our easy, simple, spontaneous action are we strong, and by contenting ourselves with obedience we become divine. Belief and love—a believing love will relieve us of a vast load of care. O my brothers, God exists.

—RALPH WALDO EMERSON (1803–1882, United States)

This one fact the world hates, that the soul becomes; for that forever degrades the past, turns all riches to poverty, all reputation to a shame, confounds the saint with the rogue, shoves Jesus and Judas equally aside.

—RALPH WALDO EMERSON (1803–1882, United States)

I am a part of all that I have met.

—LORD ALFRED TENNYSON (1809–1892, England)

Those who love God are those whom God loves.

—SUFI SAYING

In eternity there is indeed something true and sublime. But all these times and places and occasions are now and here. God himself culminates in the present moment and will never be more divine in the lapse of all the ages. Time is but a stream I go a-fishing in. I drink at it, but when I drink, I see the sandy bottom and detect how shallow it is. Its thin current slides away but eternity remains.

—HENRY DAVID THOREAU (1817–1862, United States)

The being who has attained harmony, and every being may attain it, has found his place in the order of the universe and represents the divine thought as clearly as a flower or a solar system. Harmony seeks nothing outside itself. It is what it ought to be; it is the expression of right, order, law, and truth; it is greater than time and represents eternity.

—HENRI AMIEL (1821–1881, Switzerland)

What is life? It is the flash of a firefly in the night. It is the breath of a buffalo in the wintertime; it is the little shadow which runs across the grass and loses itself in the sunset.

—CROWFOOT, CHIEF OF THE SIKSIKA FIRST NATION
(1830–1890, Canada)

The waters know their own, and draw
The brook that springs in yonder heights;
So flows the good with equal law
Unto the soul of pure delights.

The stars come nightly to the sky;
The tidal wave comes to the sea;
Nor time, nor space, nor deep, nor high,
Can keep my own away from me.

—JOHN BURROUGHS (1837–1921, United States)

When we try to pick out anything by itself, we find it
hitched to everything else in the universe.

—JOHN MUIR (1838–1918, United States)

The infinite seeks the intimate presence of the finite, the
finite to disappear in the infinite. I do not know whose
scheme this is, that the bound should be on a search for freedom, freedom asking to be housed in the bound.

—RABINDRANATH TAGORE (1861–1941, India)

Nothing is hidden from him who overcomes himself. Into
the cause of causes shalt thou penetrate, and lifting, one after
another, every veil of illusion, shalt reach at last the inmost
Heart of Being. Thus becoming one with Life, thou shalt know
all life, and, seeing into causes, and knowing realities, thou shalt
be no more anxious about thyself, and others, and the world, but
shalt see that all things that are, are engines of the Great Law.

—JAMES ALLEN (1864–1912, England)

That which is real cannot be destroyed, but only that which is unreal. When a man finds that within him which is real, which is constant, abiding, changeless, and eternal, he enters into that Reality, and becomes meek. All the powers of darkness will come against him, but they will do him no hurt, and will at last depart from him.

—JAMES ALLEN (1864–1912, England)

Man is a symbol of the laws of creation; in him there is evolution, involution, struggle, progress and retrogression, struggle between positive and negative, active and passive, yes and no, good and evil.

—GEORGE GURDJIEFF (ca. 1872–1949, Caucasus region)

Only the illimitable permanent is here. A Peace stupendous, featureless, still replaces all, what once was I, in it a silent unnamed emptiness content either to fade in the unknowable or thrill with the luminous seas of the Infinite.

—SRI AUROBINDO (1872–1950, Calcutta, India)

You come and go. The doors swing closed
ever more gently, almost without a shudder.
Of all who move through the quiet houses,

you are the quietest.
We become so accustomed to you,
we no longer look up
when your shadow falls over the book we are reading
and makes it glow. For all things
sing you: at times
we just hear them more clearly.

—RAINER MARIA RILKE (1875–1926, Bohemia)

As far as we can discern, the sole purpose of human existence
is to kindle a light in the darkness of mere being. It may even
be assumed that just as the unconscious affects us, so the
increase in our consciousness affects the unconscious.

—CARL JUNG (1875–1961, Switzerland)

For most people, even for educated and thinking people, the
chief obstacle in the way of acquiring self-consciousness
consists in the fact that they think they possess it, that is
that already they possess self-consciousness and everything
connected with it; individuality in the sense of a permanent
and unchangeable I, will, ability to do, and so on. It is evident
that a man will not be interested if you tell him that he can
acquire by long and difficult work something which, in his
opinion, he already has. On the contrary he will think either

that you are mad or that you want to deceive him with a view to personal gain.

—P. D. OUSPENSKY (1878–1947, Russia)

The true value of a human being can be found in the degree to which he has attained liberation from the self.

—ALBERT EINSTEIN (1879–1955, Germany)

Everything has its wonders, even darkness and silence, and I learn, whatever state I may be in, therein to be content.

—HELEN KELLER (1880–1968, United States)

When your presence flooded me with its light, I hoped that within it I might find Ultimate Reality at its most tangible. But now that I have in fact laid hold on you, you who are utter consistency, and feel myself borne by you I realize that my deepest hidden desire was not to possess you, but to be possessed.

—PIERRE TEILHARD DE CHARDIN (1881–1955, France)

Like the monist I plunge into the all-inclusive One; But the one is so perfect that as it receives me and I lose myself in it, I can find in it the ultimate perfection of my own individuality.

—PIERRE TEILHARD DE CHARDIN (1881–1955, France)

You often say, "I would give, but only to the deserving."
The trees in your orchard say not so,
Nor the flocks in your pastures.
They give that they may live, for to withhold is to perish.

—KAHLIL GIBRAN (1883–1931, Lebanon)

In the presence of greater meaning all lesser meanings, that
fill our ordinary mind full to the brim, shrink to their true
proportions and cease to steal from us. For in the presence of
greater meaning we are redeemed from everything small and
trivial and absurd.

—MAURICE NICOLL (1884–1953, Scotland)

A physicist is just an atom's way of looking at itself.

—NIELS BOHR (1885–1962, Denmark)

You never enjoy the world aright, till the Sea itself
floweth in your veins, till you are clothed with the heav-
ens, and crowned with the stars: and perceive yourself
to be the sole heir of the whole world, and more than so,
because men are in it who are every one sole heirs as well
as you.

—W. J. TURNER (1889–1946, Australia)

We invent nothing. We borrow and re-create. We uncover and discover. All has been given . . . we have only to open our eyes and our hearts to become one with that which is.

—HENRY MILLER (1891–1980, United States)

God is the mirror of silence in which all creation is reflected.

—PARAMAHANSA YOGANANDA (1893–1952, India)

The mirror is thoroughly egoless and mindless. If a flower comes, it reflects a flower; if a bird comes, it reflects a bird. It shows a beautiful object as beautiful, an ugly object as ugly. Everything is revealed as it is. There is no discriminating mind or self-consciousness on the part of the mirror. If something comes, the mirror reflects; if it disappears, the mirror just lets it disappear . . . no traces of anything are left behind. Such nonattachment, the state of no-mind, or the truly free working of a mirror is compared here to the pure and lucid wisdom of Buddha.

—ZENKEI SHIBAYAMA (1894–1974, Japan)

As one beholds through a small window
A single green leaf, a small patch of the vast blue sky,
So I began to perceive Thee, in the beginning of all things.

As the leaf faded and withered, the patch covered as with
dark cloud,
So didst Thou fade and vanish,
But to be reborn again,
As the single green leaf, as the small patch of the blue sky.
For many lives have I seen the bleak winter and the green
spring.
Prisoned in my little room,
I could not behold the entire tree nor the whole sky.
I swore there was no tree nor the vast sky—
That was the Truth.
Through time and destruction
My window grew large.
I beheld,
Now,
A branch with many leaves,
And a greater patch of the blue, with many clouds.
I forgot the single green leaf, the small patch of the vast blue.
I swore there was no tree, nor the immense sky—
That was the Truth.
Weary of this prison,
This small cell,
I raged at my window.
With bleeding fingers
I tore away brick after brick, I beheld,
Now,
The entire tree, its great trunk,
Its many branches, and its thousand leaves,

And an immense part of the sky.
I swore there was no other tree, no other part to the sky—
That was the Truth.
This prison no longer holds me,
I flew away through the window,
O friend,
I behold every tree and the vast expanse of the limitless sky.
Though I live in every single leaf and in every small patch of
the vast blue sky,
Though I live in every prison, looking out through every
small casement,
Liberated am I.
Lo! not a thing shall bind me—
This is the Truth.

—J. Krishnamurti (1895–1986, India)

No announcements tell the world that he has come into
enlightenment. No heralds blow the trumpets proclaiming
man's greatest victory—over himself. This is in fact the quietest moment of his whole life.

—Paul Brunton (1898–1981, England)

Pick a flower on Earth and you move the farthest star.

—Paul Dirac (1902–1984, Great Britain)

Survival is the second law of life. The first is that we are all one.

—JOSEPH CAMPBELL (1904–1987, United States)

When the next step comes, you do not take the step, you do not know the transition, you do not fall into anything. You do not go anywhere, and so you do not know the way by which you got there or the way by which you come back afterwards. You are certainly not lost. You do not fly. There is no space, or there is all space: it makes no difference.

The next step is not a step.

You are not transported from one degree to another.

What happens is that the separate entity that was you suddenly disappears and nothing is left but a pure freedom indistinguishable from infinite Freedom, love identified with love. Not two loves, one waiting for the other, striving for the other, seeking for the other, but Love Loving in Freedom.

—THOMAS MERTON (1915–1968, France)

God calls the heart and makes it exult; then he disappears; and then he reveals himself again. By the test of renunciation and a more lively "feeling" of God, a person escapes gradually from the attacks of evil: light penetrates and protects his or her nature more and more. But God refuses to provide an overwhelming proof of his presence. If he did, he would actually be destroying the very possibility of a meeting and the free offer of his love. God introduces the soul that has been made holy to a rhythm of alternate ecstasy and ecstasy, of contentment and of a yearning for an irreducible otherness, so that the soul does not cease to renew its love and spread itself in the inexhaustible store of God's riches.

—OLIVIER CLEMENT (1921–2009, France)

The mystics of all traditions speak one and the same language, the language of religious experience.

—BROTHER DAVID STEINDL-RAST (1926–, Australia)

Darkness cannot drive out darkness; only light can do that. Hate cannot drive out hate; only love can do that.

—MARTIN LUTHER KING JR. (1929–1968, United States)

We don't have to quarrel about a word, because "God" is only a word, a concept. One never quarrels about reality; we only quarrel about opinions, about concepts, about judgments. Drop your concepts, drop your opinions, drop your prejudices, drop your judgments, and you will see that.

—ANTHONY DE MELLO (1931–1987, British India)

God is like a mirror. The mirror never changes but everybody who looks at it sees something different.

—RABBI HAROLD KUSHNER (1935–, United States)

We can live without religion and meditation, but we cannot survive without affection.

—TENZIN GYATSO, 14TH DALAI LAMA (1935–, Tibet)

It is an extraordinary fact and an extraordinary piece of evidence for the truth of religion, that long hours spent in silent communication with God who never directly answers is nevertheless manifestly a two-way communication. Such a person is gradually and permanently altered in the depths of his personality in ways which would be inconceivable if there was really "nothing there" at all.

—CLIFFORD LONGLEY (1940–, England)

When you know that you are eternal, you can play your true role in time. When you know you are divine, you can become completely human. When you know you are one with God, you are free to become absolutely yourself, individual and holy and my child.

—MOTHER MEERA (1960–, India)

Don't stand by my grave and weep, for I am not there. I do not sleep. I am 1,000 winds that blow. I'm the diamond's glint on the snow. I am the sunlight on ripened grain. I am the gentle autumn's rain. Don't stand by my grave and cry. I am not there. I did not die.

—NATIVE AMERICAN POEM

Truth is one; the sages call it by many names.

—HINDU SAYING

REALIZE YOUR REAL NAME

Once upon a time a little Being was sitting by a stream . . . sighing, sad, and just a bit frightened. At that same moment, as the fates would have it, Solomon, the wise old owl, happened to be flying by just overhead.

During his many years of watching over the well-being of the forest for all the creatures living there, he had been of assistance in quite a few situations similar to this one. Solomon knew he could help this little Being . . . *if* she wished it. And so, with a turn of his head and a slight banking of his great wings, he swept down and landed, ever so lightly, alongside a small log upon which the little Being was seated. To make sure his arrival wasn't too startling, he began quietly speaking to her even before he'd finished folding back his wings.

"My, my, little one," he said in the most gentle tone, "What on earth could be making you feel so sad?"

But the little Being didn't even look up from the ground, let alone speak. So Solomon just acted as though she had answered him, and continued on in a most congenial manner. . . . "Oh, yes," he said. "Yes, for sure; I know exactly how you feel." Again he waited for her to at least acknowledge his presence—but still nothing.

"You know," he said, "there are times when it helps to speak with a friend about one's troubles . . . especially if that someone happens to know something about them . . . which . . ." He paused just long enough to make sure he had her attention, "it just so happens, I do."

Another moment passed between them, and then, ever so slowly, the little Being turned her head to look up at Solomon. Their eyes met, and he smiled into hers. She must have seen something in his face, because she took a deep breath and started to speak.

"All I want is to be happy with myself. Is that asking for too much? The other creatures seem content with themselves, but this feeling never seems to last for me; something always comes along to spoil it." And then, dropping her head into her little hands, she cried, "What on earth is wrong with me?"

"Nothing is wrong with *you*, little one. But, I do suspect—"

"Then why," she interrupted, "do so many little things bother me? How come no one seems to understand or appreciate me for who I am? And then there's this terrible need to prove myself to everyone, not to mention the fear that . . ."

Solomon had heard enough. He stepped into her stream of thought, "Hold on just a moment, little one; let's not get ahead of ourselves. If I'm to help you understand this sorrow of yours—as I'm pretty sure I can—then don't you think we should introduce ourselves? Wouldn't that be a good place to start?" And without waiting for her to agree, he said, "My name is Solomon . . . pleased to meet you! What's yours?"

Realizing he was right, the little Being gathered herself and, sitting up straight, said in a small voice, "My name is Someone."

"Really?" said Solomon. "Now isn't *that* an interesting name! Was it given to you at birth?"

"I really don't recall," she said somewhat timidly. "But I don't think so."

"Then how did you come to be called Someone? Who gave it to you?"

His question took her by surprise. No one she'd ever met had asked her anything like that before.

"Actually, it's all a little bit foggy, but one day I found myself wandering through some deep woods. I remember wondering at the time how I'd gotten there, and even who I was." Then, realizing how confused her story must sound to a complete stranger, she glanced up at Solomon to see his response. But he didn't seem surprised at all. After a deep breath, she continued on: "It was right about then that I had the good fortune of bumping into a very helpful crow by the name of Magnus. He must have known me from some time or place before, because, when

I told him of my confusion, he was kind enough to tell me my name."

Managing a small smile, she looked up at Solomon, awaiting a smile in return. But, if he was happy, he sure wasn't showing it.

"Hmm, yes . . . just as I suspected," Solomon said in tones that troubled her.

"What does *that* mean?" said the little Being, slightly on the defensive.

"I think I see your problem. I know why you've been unable to get along with the other creatures, and what's keeping you from being happy with yourself."

The little Being wasn't at all sure she liked where this conversation was headed. She had no interest in hearing Solomon remind her of what she already knew, but after a moment she went ahead and asked anyway. The unin-tended sarcasm in her own voice startled her.

"And just *what* would that be?"

Solomon paused, choosing his words carefully. Finally, he replied in measured, gentle tones, "Little one, you've been lied to . . . about your name; it isn't what you were told."

Of all the answers she could have imagined, this was the least likely. She felt a jolt—a small shock—pass through her, and her heart raced in uneven beats. And then, catching her breath—that she hadn't even noticed had gone missing—she swallowed hard and asked, "What on earth do you mean, I was lied to about my name? If my name isn't 'Someone'. . ., then what is it?"

"Your real name is *Everyone*."

IN CLOSING

LET THE WAVES WASH AWAY THE SHORES OF
YOUR SOUL

There is a storehouse of Sanity,
A vault of Love,
A treasure of Kindness,
All bursting at their seams.
Can't you feel the pressure
To just be Light?
Don't the walls of your heart
Ache to break loose and open
The floodgates of Freedom?
You have riches untold,
But have lost the map to the upper regions of yourself
Where you are always overflowing.
So, forget this world with its intermittent streams
Whose waters begin and end.
Search out the Ocean, and stand in Her surge
Until the waves wash away the shores of your soul.

—GUY FINLEY (1949–)

BIBLIOGRAPHY

The following list of books and authors presents only a small portion of the resources utilized in this collection of quotations. The majority of the material presented in this work was collected over a period exceeding thirty years and came into the author's hands through a host of different sources, including friends along the way, letters from readers, and a countless list of varied publications.

Allen, James. *As a Man Thinketh.* Santa Fe: Sun Books, 1983.

Bennett, J. G. *Deeper Man.* Santa Fe: Bennett Books, 1994.

Bloom, Harold, and Marvin Meyer. *The Gospel of St. Thomas.* San Francisco: HarperSanFrancisco, 1992.

Boehme, Jacob. *Jacob Boehme: Life and Doctrines.* Blauvelt, NY: Steiner Books, 1977.

Bucke, Richard Maurice. *Cosmic Consciousness.* New York: Penguin Books, 1969.

Bullett, Gerald. *The Testament of Light.* Avenel, NJ: Wings Books, 1994.

Clement, Olivier. *The Roots of Christian Mysticism.* New York: New City Press, 1995.

Collin, Rodney. *The Mirror of Light.* Boston: Shambhala, 1959.

de Salzmann, Jeanne. *The Reality of Being.* Boston: Shambala, 2010.

Eckhart, Meister. *Meister Eckhart, From Whom God Hid Nothing: Sermons, Writings, and Sayings.* Edited by David O'Neal. Boston: Shambhala, 1996.

Emerson, Ralph Waldo. *Selected Essays of Ralph Waldo Emerson.* New York: Penguin Books, 1984.

Gilbert, Mark. *Wisdom of the Ages.* Garden City, NY: Garden City Publications, 1936.

Gurdjieff, G. I. *Meetings with Remarkable Men.* New York: E.P. Dutton & Co., 1969.

Guyon, Jeanne. *Genesis.* Auburn, ME: Christian Books, 1972.

Hartmann, Franz. *Personal Christianity, A Science: The Doctrines of Jacob Boehme, the God-Taught Philosopher* (1919). Kessinger Publishing House, 2004.

The Holy Bible: King James Version. New York: Cambridge University Press, 1980.

Howard, Vernon. *The Mystic Masters Speak.* Boulder City, NV: New Life Books, 1974.

———. *The Power of Your Supermind.* Englewood Cliffs, NJ: Prentice Hall, 1988.

James, William. *The Varieties of Religious Experience.* New York: Penguin Books, 1982.

Krishnamurti, J. *Early Writings, Vol. 7.* Bombay, India: Chetana, 1971.

———. *The Flame of Attention.* San Francisco: Harper & Row, 1984.

Leary, William. *The Hidden Bible.* New York: C&R Anthony, 1952.

Morris, Audrey Stone. *One Thousand Inspirational Things.* New York: Hawthorne Books, 1951.

Nicoll, Maurice. *Psychological Commentaries on the Teachings of Gurdjieff & Ouspensky.* York Beach, ME: Weiser, 1980.

———. *The New Man.* Utrecht, the Netherlands: Eureka Edition, 1999.

Ouspensky, P. D. *The Fourth Way.* New York: Vintage Books, 1971.

———. *In Search of the Miraculous.* New York: Harvest/HBJ Books, 1976.

Rilke, Rainer Maria. *Rilke on Love and Other Difficulties.* Edited by John L. Mood. New York: W. W. Norton & Co., 1995.

Saint Augustine and R. S. Pine-Coffin. *Confessions.* New York: Dorset Press, 1986.

Schimmel, Annemarie. *I Am Light, You Are Fire: The Life and Works of Rumi.* New York: W. W. Norton, 1975.

Thoreau, Henry David. *Walden.* Boston: Shambhala, 1992.

Tozer, A. W. *Men Who Met God.* Camp Hill, PA: Christian Publications, 1986.

Underhill, Evelyn. *Mystics of the Church.* Harrisburg, PA: Morehouse Publications, 1995.

Watson, Lillian. *Light from Many Lamps: A Treasury of Inspiration.* New York: Simon and Schuster, 1951.

Watts, Alan. *In My Own Way.* Novato, CA: New World Library, 1972.

Wright, Louis B., and Virginia A. LaMar. *The Play's the Thing.* New York: Harper & Row, 1963.

ABOUT THE AUTHOR

© MINDI MORGAN

Guy Finley is the founder and director of the nonprofit Life of Learning Foundation, a world-renowned school for self-realization. He has been helping individuals find a life of uncompromised freedom and enduring fulfillment for thirty years.

Finley is a spiritual teacher who distills the wisdom of the ages and makes it accessible to all. A modern-day master, he is the best-selling author of more than forty books and unique audio albums, including *The Courage to Be Free*, *The Essential Laws of Fearless Living*, *Let Go and Live in the Now*, *The Secret of Letting Go*, and *Liberate Your Self*. He also regularly conducts workshops and intensives at the Omega Institute, Kripalu, and other major spiritual centers.

Visit his foundation online at *www.guyfinley.org* and subscribe to his free weekly e-newsletter.

To write the author about this book, receive information about his ongoing classes, or request a catalog of his works (along with a free study guide), send a self-addressed stamped envelope to:

Guy Finley
P.O. Box 10–S
Merlin, OR 97532
Phone: 541-476-1200

A SPECIAL FREE GIFT

FOR BUYERS OF *THE SEEKER, THE SEARCH, THE SACRED*

THE FOUR FUNDAMENTAL PRINCIPLES OF SPIRITUAL FREEDOM

A new breakthrough 60-minute DVD from best-selling author Guy Finley. Includes FREE shipping.*

This transformational DVD will introduce you to the beautiful, higher mind that already dwells within you so that you can know its perfect judgment, effortless intuition, tireless compassion, and spontaneous creativity. Once you realize its infinite possibilities:

- Your direct contact with higher wisdom will give you a deeper, clearer understanding in every moment.

- Your relationships will be more true, more loving, and less complicated.

- You will have a greater sense of serenity and security.

* Free shipping offer valid for addresses in the U.S. only. This is a limited time offer and is subject to change. Please see Guy Finley's website for further information and restrictions.

- You will experience new impressions and energies.
- You will have the power to meet each moment, whatever it may bring—and transform it for the good of everyone.

Awaken your true capabilities and build the foundation for greater well-being and fulfillment. Request your FREE copy of *The Four Fundamental Principles of Spiritual Freedom* by Guy Finley today.

Visit *www.guyfinley.org/SeekerDVD* or call (541) 476-1200 to request your FREE DVD today!

TO OUR READERS

Weiser Books, an imprint of Red Wheel/Weiser, publishes books across the entire spectrum of occult, esoteric, speculative, and New Age subjects. Our mission is to publish quality books that will make a difference in people's lives without advocating any one particular path or field of study. We value the integrity, originality, and depth of knowledge of our authors.

Our readers are our most important resource, and we appreciate your input, suggestions, and ideas about what you would like to see published.

Visit our website *www.redwheelweiser.com* where you can subscribe to our newsletters and learn about our upcoming books, exclusive offers, and free downloads.

You can also contact us at *info@redwheelweiser.com* or at

Red Wheel/Weiser, LLC
665 Third Street, Suite 400
San Francisco, CA 94107